LIFE
is for Living

LIFE
is for Living

an introductory guide to living the Christian life

Peter J. Horrobin

Marshalls

Marshalls Paperbacks
Marshall Morgan & Scott
3 Beggarwood Lane, Basingstoke, Hants, RG23 7LP, UK

First published by Marshall Pickering Communications Ltd.

British Library CIP data
Horrobin, Peter
Life is for living.
1. Christian life——1960–
I. Title
248.4   BV4501.2

ISBN 0–551–01173–4

Typeset by Wyvern Typesetting Ltd, Bristol
Printed in Great Britain by
Anchor Brendon Ltd, Tiptree, Essex

For Margaret, Anne and Mark

Contents

Foreword

It was through Mission England that Peter Horrobin and I first met. He was to become one of the most supportive and caring friends I have ever found.

It is this caring and supportive quality that runs right through this book. Peter is writing for the person who has just opened his or her heart and mind to the reality of Jesus Christ. He recognises that for such a person everything can seem pretty bewildering.

Peter's concern goes beyond mere survival of such a person in the 'brave new world'. He wants to see growth and maturity. The sooner every new believer finds his or her feet as a contributing Christian in the church and in the world, the better for all concerned. With the great evangelistic missions of 1984 so close behind us, and with all that has happened since – there is no shortage of people who need to read a book like this – thank the Lord!

A friend of mine is fond of saying that the churches tend to make new Christians prisoners of war, when they should be treating them as recruits in the army. Everyone who takes sides with Christ will soon find there's a war on and that you can't be neutral!

I long to see new Christians finding a welcome and a warm place in the congregation. But more than that – I long to see such people sharing their new-found faith with their friends and contacts from pre-Christian days. As St. Matthew discovered, the best time to start sharing Christ is the day that you meet Him!

I'm sure that Peter's book will help many that have recently put their trust in Christ. Peter tries to be realistic about the world around us. He tries to be realistic also about the churches (he lets a few of the warts show!). Most of all he tries to be realistic about the resources God offers the Christian through His Holy Spirit. On this last point he is anxious to talk about such matters as Spiritual gifts from square one in the new Christian's experience so as to avoid some of the problems which arise when we try to nurture new Christians as if there wasn't a Holy Spirit, thus leaving them a prey to the weirdest of views later on. I'm sure he is right to try to do this.

I hope and pray that this book will bring understanding, strength and guidance to many people.

Gavin Reid
National Director of Mission England

Preface

The purpose of this book is simple: to help new Christians live the Christian life. Their new life has to be lived in the real world and it is not always easy for them to find answers to the problems they face. They are often confused by what they find inside the fellowship of a local church. And they usually need help in getting sensible routines established in their lives which will help their faith to grow.

I trust that the book will be helpful also to those who have the responsibility of caring for new Christians, as well as older Christians who are now struggling in the faith because they did not have the benefit of practical advice and teaching when they first committed their lives to Christ.

The book has been designed in a logical sequence so that it can be read right through. But each chapter is also complete in itself, so if a reader wants to study one particular chapter he can understand it without having to refer to all the others. Because of this some important points, which are relevant to more than one chapter, are sometimes repeated.

The content of the book draws heavily on the Bible, but only in a very few places has the text been broken up by the addition of Bible references. Again, this is deliberate, so that those who are not used to reading Christian books will not feel that they are being faced with a study course which is beyond their desire or experience.

At the end of the book there is an appendix of scripture references which is compiled so that those who want to read further will quickly be able to find the relevant passages of scripture. This will also be useful for those who need material to form the basis of a fellowship meeting or group Bible study. The second appendix will help new Christians understand the difference between the various denominations.

I pray that as this book is read, it will be used by God to encourage Christians in their faith as they seek to become living witnesses to the hope that is in them.

Peter J. Horrobin

Acknowledgements

This book could not have been completed without the help of many people. I would like to thank: Pat Hodgson, who typed the manuscript – not once, but several times, has never complained and frequently made important contributions to the text; Rebecca Harris, who read and constructively criticised the original manuscript, introduced new ideas and compiled the appendix of scripture references; Derek Simpson, who made many helpful comments on the manuscript; Gavin Reid, who not only read and commented on the text, but also contributed the Foreword; numerous other friends who helped by reading and commenting on sections of the manuscript or checking proofs; and my family who were patient throughout it all!

Chapter 1

From Death to Life

The Step You Have Taken

Recently I went canoeing for the first time. The inevitable happened. There was a collision, I lost my balance and the next thing I remember was hanging upside down, from the canoe, under the water. I am a tall man, my legs are long and for a few seconds I couldn't extract them from the capsized canoe. I was trapped.

Suddenly my legs came free, my life-jacket did its job, and, much to my relief, my head popped up above the water. The crisis was over. My family tell me that there wasn't really any danger as there was an experienced instructor and life-saver close to hand. But no amount of assurance on this point could take away the experience of facing the possibility of death.

The consequences of death are only fully appreciated when they stare you in the face. But when the crisis is over the ordinary activities of life very quickly assume greater priority. We don't like to think too long or too hard about the fact of death. But, in life, bodily death is the only thing we can look forward to with absolute certainty!

So, when Jesus told his followers 'I have come that you might have life – life in all its fulness' He was speaking about a subject which is of vital concern to every single person. For life is the only antidote to death. And for all who know Jesus, death is no longer an enemy to be feared but a gateway to a new life.

You may only have been a Christian for a very short time, or you may have been a believer for many years – the length of time since your conversion is irrelevant. What matters is that you have taken that tremendous step *from death to LIFE* – a life which you can enjoy now and which will continue beyond the grave.

Most of this book is about living the Christian life, but it is often the case that new Christians (as well as some older Christians!) are still confused about what has happened to them. So we will spend the rest of this chapter making sure that we understand what it means to be a Christian.

One of the expressions that is used to describe what happens when you become a Christian is 'to be born again'. Jesus used this phrase Himself when explaining to Nicodemus how it was possible for a man to get to know God (John 3). Another word which describes the same experience is 'conversion'. Conversion, therefore, is a new birth. This is the first of five new things which we will look at to help us answer the question 'What is a Christian?'

1. A New Birth

The Bible describes man as having three components: body, soul (personality) and spirit. We have no difficulty in understanding what our body is. If we tread on an upturned drawing pin in bare feet we know all too quickly that we have one. All our bodies are conveniently different – they come in many shapes, sizes and complexions and each one is unique.

But when we talk about our bodies we do so in a language which betrays the fact that our soul has a completely separate existence from the body. If a man loses his leg in an accident it only affects his body – he is still the same person. It is our soul which gives our personalities those unique qualities which ensure no one could ever mistake us for someone else even if our bodies looked very alike.

The Bible tells us, however, that God made us in His

own image. And Jesus explained how God is spirit and those who worship Him must do so in spirit and in truth. So, it would seem reasonable to expect that as well as a body and a soul, man should also have a spirit with which to enjoy a relationship with the God who created him. It is this spirit which completes man in the image of God and makes him unique from the rest of creation – with a body to live in, a soul which gives to each individual a unique personality and a spirit with which to enjoy a relationship with God the Father who created us.

On these matters the Bible speaks very clearly. It tells us:

1. Everyone's body will die.
2. Everyone's soul will not die but carry on living beyond the grave.
3. Everyone's spirit is dead (to God) because of sin – rebellion against God. (The source of this rebellion and the nature of sin is explained on page 32.)
4. Whilst the spirit is dead to God it is impossible to have a relationship with Him. The consequence of sin is eternal banishment from the presence of a loving and holy God.
5. We can never take our place in the Kingdom of God unless our spirit is brought back to life (born again). For this to happen the cause of our spirit's death (sin) must be dealt with.
6. Jesus, who never sinned, dealt with our sin on the cross. He took upon Himself the punishment that should have been ours – banishment from the presence of God. On the cross Jesus cried out in anguish, 'My God, My God, why have You forsaken Me?' At death, he experienced the reality of being banished from the presence of God.
7. Jesus was not left by God to live out eternity in hell but, having experienced the consequences of our sin and paid the necessary price for it, God raised Him from the dead.

8.   If we believe that Jesus' death was on our behalf and realise that there is no other way that our sin can be dealt with, we can then turn to God in repentance. Because of Jesus' death, God forgives us and cleanses us from our sin. With the same power with which He raised Jesus from death, God then brings new life to our spirit by sending the Holy Spirit to live within us.

9.   This new life of God within us makes us children of God and restores the relationship that God intended for us when we were created; that we should know Him and love Him 'with all our heart, with all our soul and with all our strength'. For this, Jesus said, *is* eternal life, that we might 'know the one true God, and Jesus Christ whom He sent'.

So, it is only when our spirit is born again that we experience the new birth. We are born again by faith in Jesus Christ when we turn to Him as Saviour (from the consequences of our sin). 'For God loved the world so much that He gave His only Son that every one who believes in Him should not perish but have eternal life' (John 3:16).

Nothing that happens to you in the future can break the relationship you now have with God the Father. For example, my own son will always be *my* son. Nothing he can ever do will change the nature of our relationship. But there may well be times when we do not enjoy our relationship. Such as, if he were to deliberately disobey an important instruction I had given him. I would be deeply hurt that his love for me was not a sufficient motive for ensuring his obedience.

As a Christian you have the Holy Spirit of God in your heart and you also have the written word of God (the Bible) to read and understand. As a result you will know when you are being tempted to do wrong. When you give in to the temptation, you sin, but you do not *break* the relationship you have with God. God is hurt when sin interferes in the relationship, and your fellowship with

14

Him is spoiled. Restoration of the fellowship (which characterises a relationship with God) is only achieved by both telling God with your lips that you are sorry (confession) and actually being sorry in your life by putting right in a practical way anything that has happened as a result of your disobedience.

Do not worry if at this point you don't understand all of this – you don't need to be able to understand it all with your mind in order to experience Jesus Christ in your life. But it is important that you believe it. If you understand that you are a sinner, have confessed your sin, asked God to forgive you and asked Jesus Christ into your life as your Lord and Saviour, that is enough. God will help you to understand more of His truth as and when you need it.

2. A New Life

A new baby can look forward to a whole new life. As a new Christian so can you. For you are, now, a complete person. Only a Christian has all the resources for living that God intended everyone to use and enjoy. For only a Christian is complete, with a body, a soul *and* a spirit which has been made whole (from the consequences of sin) by being born again.

The primary sign of life is growth. That rule applies just as much to a Christian life as it does to the bodily life of a new born baby. Paul was the first great Christian missionary and he talked about the need for new Christians to feed on the 'milk of the Word of God'! No one would dream of asking a new born baby to survive on steak and chips and neither should you, as a new Christian, launch into heavyweight theology.

It is absolutely vital, however, that you do start reading the Bible and let God feed you with the truth of His Word. But, be wise in the things that you try to take in. In Chapter 3 you will find some practical advice about how to get going.

Then you must pray. But don't be alarmed by that thought and imagine that tomorrow morning you have to get up and pray just like the minister on television last Sunday morning. Leading prayers in public on behalf of other people is only one aspect of prayer. All you need to do at this stage is to remember that God is your Father and talk to Him naturally – again Chapter 3 will help you. The third type of food that will help you to grow is fellowship. The word fellowship means that special quality of friendship which Christians can have one with another. So, you will want to be sharing with other Christians in the life of their local church fellowship – see Chapter 4.

It will be some time before the benefits of regular feeding will be evident in a growing body. Seconds after a baby is fed is not the time to start looking for consequential growth! But if the baby was not fed, you would very quickly see a difference! In just the same way, if a new Christian does not feed on the Word of God, prayer and fellowship, in a very short period of time his Christian life will have deteriorated and other interests will have occupied the time which rightly belongs to God. Lack of spiritual food will very soon be evident.

When Paul was writing to his young friend Timothy he reminded him of the value of good food and exercise, but more than that he underlined how important it is to have the right kind of spiritual food and spiritual exercise. So don't underestimate the importance of reading your Bible, praying and sharing in the life of the local fellowship of Christians.

3. New Relationships

A growing baby gradually becomes aware of a whole range of relationships it has with other people. The number one relationship is with its parents – especially mother. A new Christian is immediately aware of a new relationship with God as he starts to experience a personal relationship with the Father from whom he has received life – both bodily life and, now, eternal spiritual life.

When Jesus was on earth He talked about God as being His Father. You now have unity with Jesus, the Son of

God, and you are able to enjoy with Him this same Fatherhood of God.

Just as human relationships can be spoiled when we let people down or unnecessarily hurt them, our relationship with God the Father can be spoiled when we do wrong (sin). When that happens to you thank God for Jesus, for He died that you might be forgiven. Confess your sin, receive God's forgiveness and continue to enjoy a restored relationship with God. One of the works of God's Holy Spirit is to make you conscious of sin – you will then know when you do wrong and your relationship with God can be immediately restored. You will find out more about this in Chapter 6 as you understand how the Holy Spirit wants to produce in you the characteristics of God Himself.

There are other aspects of new relationships that a growing child begins to experience – the wider range of family and friends who are interested in the baby's welfare. In the church, as a new Christian, you can enjoy and benefit from fellowship with the wider Christian family. That is why other Christians are sometimes referred to as brothers and sisters in Christ. They are people in whom we see the reality of Christ's presence and with whom we share the Fatherhood of God. Part of Christian growth is learning to appreciate and depend upon the wider circle of relationships that our life in Christ makes possible.

Finally, because you are a Christian, you now have something very special in common with every other Christian throughout the world. So wherever you are and whatever you are doing you have friends and can enjoy their fellowship. The Christian family is far bigger than the limits of your local horizon!

4. A New Foundation

Jesus told the story of a wise man who built a house on a rock and a foolish man who built a similar house on sand. Both houses were fine until they were tested with wind and rain. The house on the rock stood firm but the house built on sand suffered a dramatic collapse.

He then said that if you listen to what God is saying and obey Him in your life you will be like the man who built a house on the rock – you will be able to stand up to all the pressures that this world can throw at you. So, if you have trusted God's Word and become a Christian, your life is now built on a secure foundation.

Paul explained this when he was writing to his friends in the church at Corinth – he told them that God has given Jesus to us as the one and only foundation for life, and that no other foundation whatsoever is possible. Without Christ you are building on sand. With Christ your life is founded on rock.

What matters now, then, is what you build on the foundation that God has given you. The rest of this book will help you understand how to build those things that God has in His plan for your life.

5. A New Future

Depression has many causes, but one of the commonest is the deep sense of hopelessness that some people experience. It overrides every other emotion and it seems as though there is nothing to live for.

In conversation we talk about there being no hope when somebody is critically ill. A situation is described as hopeless, when, humanly speaking, the solution that people would want to see seems beyond reach. We find it easier to understand the meaning of the word hope by reference to our intuitive understanding of what it is to be without hope. For, in the Christian sense, the word hope means much, much more than, for example, 'I hope it won't rain tomorrow!' The Christian word, hope, means a definite expectation not an outside possibility.

So what are the definite expectations that as a Christian are now your hope? Some people confuse the issue by thinking that the Christian *only* has a hope of eternal life beyond the grave. That is false teaching which is a lie of the devil designed to keep Christians away from doing

18

God's work here on earth. A sense of hopelessness about the present life is often the starting point for spiritual, and even physical, depression.

Eternal life began, for you, at your conversion. From that moment on God was in your life. Physical death, when it comes, will be a transition from living your eternal life with God here on earth to living your eternal life with Him in heaven. Christianity is not just a hope-for-tomorrow religion. Nor is the hope-for-today to be interpreted as God giving us every physical enjoyment that our human desires could absorb. We would quickly become bored with selfish activity and less and less interested in our true destiny.

No, today's hope is far more satisfying than any materialistic pleasure that can be found in the world. It is the joy of knowing God; experiencing His power at work in your life; living at the centre of His will; enjoying the present because you are no longer afraid of the future; looking forward to tomorrow because Christ, the hope of the world, is alive in your heart.

God *will* allow you to enjoy many of the things that He has created in this world. But, if we seek those things in preference to the Creator, our lives will quickly get out of balance, and the hope which is a Christian's birthright will disappear over the horizon like a dream at break of day.

As a Christian you have a new future to enjoy while you are alive on earth. And you have a new future to look forward to with God in heaven. The step you have taken in becoming a Christian really *is* one from death to LIFE.

Chapter 2

Brave New World

A Brand New Look at the World
We Live In

There is a certain seaside resort which often has bad weather. On a cloudy day the grey sea is far from inviting and the view inland is very uninspiring. The town itself has little architectural character and the only bright lights are the artificial ones flashing incessantly from amusement arcades.

Recently, however, I visited the same town on a clear bright day. I was stunned by its breathtaking beauty. The sea glittered and across the bay the most magnificent range of hills and mountains provided an unsurpassable backdrop to a glorious scene.

Yes, the place was exactly the same but the clouds had lifted and the view that had been there all the time outshone the artificial attractions of an otherwise unattractive town. Because the clouds had lifted I was seeing things in a brand new way.

Becoming a Christian has the effect of lifting the clouds from our eyes so that we are able to see things in a completely new and different light. The Bible talks about 'all things becoming new' when we come to Christ. We acquire a completely new set of 'eyes' through which to see and understand the world around us. All the things we could see before are still there, but, in addition, there is much more that previously we were blind to. We have a totally new outlook on every single aspect of our lives.

In practice you will find it easier to be aware of this new perspective in life than to let its consequences be worked out in the daily routines of family relationships, work and leisure. The Holy Spirit will be constantly revealing to us God's view of each situation we face, and His way ahead for us. God has given us the free-will to choose whether or not we are going to be obedient to His revealed will; He never forces us into any particular course of action.

When we choose to go our own way we sin and a shadow is cast across our relationship with the Lord. When we realise what we have done we need to tell God we are sorry, and ask Him for forgiveness. The Apostle John was writing to Christians when he said, 'If you confess your sin, God, who is just, will forgive you' (1 John 1:9).

When you sin you may feel that you are not a Christian. The devil wants you to believe this, but it's only because you *are* a Christian that you are so conscious of your sin. God's Spirit is a *Holy* Spirit and His presence within you brings a new understanding of what is right and wrong.

Again, never believe the devil when he says that, because you have sinned, God cannot use you. Be encouraged that the very first sermon preached on the Day of Pentecost (when God gave the Holy Spirit to the church) was preached by one of Jesus's disciples, a man who only weeks earlier had denied on three separate occasions that he ever knew Jesus. God's forgiveness reaches down to the very depths of our humanity – there is no sin that is beyond His forgiveness. But never, either, let the fact of God's forgiveness be used as an excuse for continuing to indulge in known sin. That is playing with fire and denying the rights Jesus now has on your life. There are many Christians who have to be content with God's second-best in their lives because a deliberate act of sin has taken them into areas of activity which they knew were outside God's will for them.

So, if you have only just become a Christian be

determined to let the Holy Spirit have His own way in every area of your life. You will never regret it and in so doing you will experience the greatest joy imaginable.

We shall now look at some of the areas in which your way of life will be challenged (and changed) by your faith.

1. Relationships

When you became a Christian you exchanged your old life for new life in Christ. God's Holy Spirit is now at work within. Now, therefore, you no longer belong to yourself, but to God. When Paul was challenged about what a Christian should, or should not, do with regard to relationships, he replied, 'Don't you know that your body is the temple of the Holy Spirit, who lives in you and who was given to you by God? You do not belong to yourself but to God; He bought you for a price (the blood of Jesus). So use your bodies for His glory' (1 Corinthians 6:19).

That advice still holds good and it is adequate to cover all our relationship problems. We have the Holy Spirit within us. He was given to us by God. If we grieve the Holy Spirit, by ignoring His promptings, we sin and will lose our inner peace. And always remember that the Holy Spirit could never lead us into behaviour which is contrary to the will of God as written in the scriptures.

The relationships which concern us most are usually those which involve our immediate families (if we still live at home with our parents or are married), our partners (if we are living intimately with someone to whom we are not married) or other people with whom we may be involved in occasional extra-marital or other illegitimate activities. For younger people their greatest concern is often boy-friend/girlfriend relationships. Let's look first at our relationship with parents.

God's command to us is to 'honour your father and mother'. We need to ask God to help us fulfil this. Even if our parents are not Christians, God has placed them in authority over us and we must respect that and trust that God will bring any decisions they make concerning us into
22

line with His plans for our lives so that we can obey both God and our parents without conflict. This attitude of respect and willing obedience will become a tremendous witness to the reality of your Christian experience and probably provide many opportunities for you to share what Jesus has done for you.

Parents, however, have been known to put pressure on children not to get involved in church life. They are frightened that their children are being 'got at' and need protection – especially if the parents hold very strong anti-religious views themselves. Whilst this can be very hard for young people it is not a totally impossible situation, for no-one can take away their right to spend time reading the Bible and praying. If you are in this situation you will naturally be praying that God will work in your family, that your family will see what God has done in your life, and that they will be open to listen when the opportunity to share your faith arises. Be encouraged, many whole families have become Christians through the faithful testimony of one of the children!

It can be much harder when a wife or husband of a non-Christian couple is first converted. For, instead of bringing harmony into the marriage, initially Christ is often a source of division. But if the new Christian allows the Holy Spirit to produce in him or her the characteristics talked about in Chapter Five, I believe, that, in time and in answer to the prayers of the Christian, God will work actively in the life of the other partner. Conversely, there are many known situations where a particularly bad wife or husband is converted and the resulting change is so dramatic that the other partner is instantly convicted by the power and love of God and is also converted!

When it comes to extra-marital relationships or pre-marital sexual relationships the situation is clearly defined. For the Bible states quite definitely that this is a 'no-go' area for the Christian. It is God's desire that we should get the very best out of our marriage. This means that for Christians, sex is something to be enjoyed only in this context. In issues such as this do not be embarrassed or shy about seeking the practical help of an older Christian you can trust – for you may well need support in working out the consequences of changes in your conduct. Married people should ask God to renew the life of their own marriage rather than seek satisfaction elsewhere. Single people will need to seek God's help in controlling their desires until married to the person of God's choosing. The Bible tells us very plainly not to enter into an unequal relationship.

In a book of this nature we cannot discuss all the relationships that will be touched by your Christian commitment, but I do believe that if you will apply the principles of Christian living explained in this and other chapters, that you will very quickly find God leading you out of any consequential problem.

2. Time

Before you became a Christian you lived for yourself. Your time was your own and even if you made a mess of things you were master of your own life and responsible to yourself for your actions. But when you received Christ as your Saviour, you handed your life over to Him and He is your Lord. He is now living His life through you and you're living your life in His service. Your time, therefore, is now His and how you spend it matters.

The two immediate areas where there will be a difference are:

(a) on a daily basis you will be spending some time with God in prayer and reading the Bible (see Chapter 3), and

(b) on a regular basis you will be sharing with other Christians in the life of your local church fellowship – certainly on Sunday and probably one evening a week as well (see Chapter 4).

Re-arranging your schedules so as to make time for your

personal devotions will not be too difficult, although it will require discipline on your part to keep it up – especially if the rest of your family are not Christians and, because they don't understand what has happened, make something of a joke about what you are doing. Don't let that deter you from keeping to that regular time of prayer – always remember to pray very specially for your immediate family who are now being affected by the consequences of your new faith.

There will be many opportunities to talk to them about the Lord – but be careful not to 'ram religion down their throats'. God *will* give you opportunities to share your faith if you ask Him – there is no need for your witness to be forced on unwilling listeners.

You live in a real world with real people and just because you have become a Christian does not mean that all your family and friends are readily going to adjust their time-tables to free you for other activities. Instead of thinking how great it is that you have committed your life to Christ, they are much more likely to feel betrayed because something in your life has come between you and them. The re-organising of time and priorities will not be easy, but if you are to grow in the Christian life it is vital that you should make your stand for Christ as you become part of the local fellowship of Christians. Chapters 4 and 5 will help you sort out these priorities.

As well as making time for new activities arising from your Christian life, you are also going to be faced with the possibility of dropping some activities you have been involved in. You may have been used to doing something on a regular basis as a non-Christian which you now realise would be wrong to pursue. Pray about each issue, seek the advice of older Christians in your church fellowship, check to see what the Bible teaches about it, listen to the voice of the Holy Spirit and be obedient to whatever God is saying to you on the issue.

God is not a kill-joy. He does not want to take out of your life everything which you enjoy, but in many people's lives there are activities which cannot be reconciled with the Christian life and these have to go. There is no need to be proud and condemnatory in the way you withdraw from these activities – after all you supported them up to a very short time ago. But it is important that, in a simple way, you explain why you will not be involved in the future. It is not a good witness to say you no longer wish to go to the gambling casino because pigeon-racing is now your all-consuming interest! Tell the truth. God will honour you for it, He has promised in His Word that He will honour those who honour Him. Whilst people are unlikely to agree with you instantaneously – they will have a sneaking regard for you and something of your testimony will have made its mark.

3. Sundays

On Sundays you may well find that your desire to go to the Sunday services at your local church will seriously conflict with what the rest of your family and friends want to do. It may be that you've always been used to playing a game of squash at 11 am on a Sunday morning, visiting relatives for lunch, cutting the grass, playing Monopoly with the children, or . . . one could go on, for there is a variety of things that people do on a Sunday which involve other people.

Most of the early Christians were Jews and for them the Sabbath (Saturday) was a special day set apart for God. As the Church expanded and incorporated new Christians from many different backgrounds, Sunday was gradually established as the special day set apart by Christians as their holy day. Sunday, the first day of the week, was chosen to commemorate the day on which Jesus was raised from the dead.

God promised the Jews many blessings if they would use the Sabbath correctly. It has always been assumed that these blessings can also be claimed by Christians, even though the day they have set apart is a different one from the Jewish Sabbath. Certainly I can confirm the truth of
26

this from my own experience.

However, there has grown up around the Christian Sunday the myth that this is a day on which you 'don't do things'. To a certain extent this may be true, but it is a pity that *the whole truth* has not been fully appreciated, that far from being a day on which you don't do things, it is a day that you do completely different things and there is no time, therefore, for irrelevant activity.

For Sunday is a day set apart for God. A day when we spend time with other Christians in fellowship at our church services. A day when we spend time with our families without the daily pressures of the working week. A day when there is greater opportunity for praying and reading the Bible. A day for appreciating God in every area of our lives. If we do use Sunday effectively there will just not be time for all the other things you may usually think of doing. It is particularly important to guard this day from activities that would make it inconvenient to attend church services.

It may not be easy for you so to rearrange your activities that Sunday is free to spent in this way, but there is no doubt whatsoever that if you really do make the effort to let God use this day in your life for the maximum benefit, you will experience very considerable blessing as you grow and mature as a Christian.

4. Entertainment

An old proverb says, 'You are not what you think you are, but what you think, you are'. The things with which we fill our minds have a powerful effect on the way we live and, in time, the things that we think about will determine what we become.

Television is today's number one entertainment. Many people watch it for several hours every single day. Its power to educate is tremendous, a power that is only matched by its power to corrupt. The Christian needs to be alert to the dangers of television in two specific areas.

Firstly, in the area of morality. When television

portrays as normal the low standard (or lack) of morality of a small minority, then what was formerly considered acceptable behaviour by only a few, eventually becomes the acceptable standard and even example for the majority. The arrival of video has dramatically increased the power of television in this respect.

Entertainment, in its various forms, such as literature, the theatre, cinema etc., has often been used as a means of encouraging changes in the moral behaviour of society. For the Christian the only acceptable standards of moral behaviour are those contained in the scriptures, and we must be careful not to let what we watch on television compromise those standards. Discipline in the choice of what we watch is vital. And it is equally vital that parents should be disciplined in what they let their children watch. Their lives are being shaped by what they see and hear.

The second area in which the Christian needs to be alert to the dangers of television is with respect to how he spends his time. We only have a certain amount of time to live, and while some television programmes are important sources of information and relaxation, it is not sensible to spend ten to twenty per cent of our lives watching a screen with which it is impossible to have a meaningful relationship! The television *is* an important element in today's society, but it must be used wisely as a servant and not be allowed to become the master. There are too many Christians whose lives have headed for trouble because they did not make the time to pray, read the Bible and benefit from the fellowship of other Christians. They did, however, find the time for several hours of television every night!

At its simplest this whole problem is just a matter of discipline as we establish a wise balance between time spent in front of the television and time spent on other activities. Some people do, however, find the discipline of the on/off switch a very difficult one to enforce and you may have to fill your time positively with other beneficial activities before you get to the point of being able to watch only those programmes which are right for you. The ultimate disciplinary measure is to get rid of the television altogether! I do know of some people who have taken this step and never regretted it.

What I have said about television and video applies equally to every other form of entertainment. We must be constantly on our guard to ensure that the things we fill our minds with are wholesome, and that it is right for us to devote time to them.

5. Money

Paul said that the *love* of money is the root of all evil – not money itself. Used wisely, money can be the source of great blessing. The Bible has quite a bit to say about how a Christian should use his money. As Christians we acknowledge that everything we have now belongs to God and should be placed at His disposal; we are merely stewards of that which He has given us, and that includes our money.

It is obvious that the work of the church requires money. Full-time workers need salaries, buildings need to be maintained, evangelism needs to be financed, etc., etc. In the Old Testament God gave some very practical guidelines and rules that were to be obeyed in order that His work should not suffer through lack of financial support. He also promised that those who were obedient in this respect would not suffer themselves, but would be blessed abundantly for their faithfulness.

The rules laid down in the scripture were simple: ten per cent of all income (from whatever source) should be given for the Lord's work. This ten per cent was known as a *tithe*. Any giving over and above this was known as a *free-will offering* – implying that the tithe was an obligation about which there was no choice!

Christians who have adopted for themselves these practical guidelines for their giving have always testified to the faithfulness of God with regard to their finances. He is not in the business of letting people down who are giving precious resources for His service.

Many local churches today are so preoccupied with raising money – much of which is needed for purposes concerned with the fabric of their buildings as opposed to evangelism and meeting social needs – that the real work of the church is being stifled. If every church member took seriously God's Word to His people about giving, the church would not lack any resources for its work. For it is only a very small percentage of church members that do take the ten per cent principle seriously and an even smaller percentage that would consider giving free-will offerings over and above the ten per cent! But the implication of scripture is that if a need arises which exceeds the ten per cent we should not consider that our upper limit has been reached and say that we cannot meet this need! Nor should we pinch it from the ten per cent that would arise from future income!

May I encourage you, therefore, to start your Christian life in the way that you intend to go on and not to wait until you're better off before being obedient to God's Word. God will honour your commitment to Him as you put your finances on to a right spiritual footing. Always remember that all the resources you have (your home, your possessions, your time etc.) are a gift from God to be used for Him.

6. Language
The way people speak is often an expression of their life and personality. A person who uses the names of God and Jesus as swear words is unlikely to think very much about what it means to be a Christian. So, if, as a Christian, you are concerned to witness for your faith to others and at the same time you decorate your conversation with blasphemous language, your testimony is not going to sound very convincing. Your listeners will rightly condemn you as a hypocrite.

The Bible teaches us to speak graciously, without

swearing. Accordingly, this sort of language should be the norm for every Christian. Swearing includes the supposedly more acceptable expletives as well as the many words in common usage of sexual origin.

Lips that are used to praise and worship God should not also be used for blasphemy. But old habits die hard and if you work in an atmosphere where bad language is expected you will find it especially difficult. Do pray for God's power to overcome this and to break the habit. One thing is certain, by ceasing to swear your testimony will be noticed!

7. Truthfulness

When Jesus claimed to be The Truth, He was declaring the fact that He was the Son of God and every single thing He said and did could be trusted and relied upon. He could not deceive anyone. When you became a Christian the Holy Spirit started work in your life to reproduce in you the characteristics of Jesus, and day-by-day, as you give the Holy Spirit permission to deal with you, that is just what He will do.

Specifically He will give you the desire to be truthful in all you think, say and do. And that means being true to your commitment to God, being true to yourself and being utterly truthful in all your dealings with others.

Whilst chemists may be in the drug business, mechanics in the motor business, Christians are in the truth business. And there are times when you'll find the truth hurts – for, there may well be occasions when, on the face of it, it will be costly to tell the truth and not deceive people. Do not let this deter you from being faithful to your commitment.

There are times when we all face acute temptation in some area of our life. If anyone were to ask us questions about our behaviour we would, because we are Christians, have to be honest in our reply. This has a significant strengthening effect on our resolve not to succumb to that temptation. A commitment to truthfulness is a powerful ally!

8. Satan, Sin and the Occult World

Before God created man He created the angels – heavenly beings whose purpose was to serve God and minister to Him. The Bible tells us how the chief of these angels rebelled against God, deciding to set up a kingdom in opposition to God's and make himself equal to God as the head of this kingdom. God dealt with this rebellion by casting that angel (now called Satan), out of Heaven. With him went other angelic spirits (now known as demons or evil spirits) who joined in the rebellion. Jesus described this in Luke, Chapter 10. Satan now reigns as the prince of darkness until, at the end of the age, his power will be utterly destroyed by God. From the very beginning his whole objective has been to drag others into his rebellion so that they will worship him instead of the living God.

God made us in His own image, and among other things, that means we were given a spirit with which to communicate with God. Many people feel the need to satisfy this spiritual dimension but have never been confronted with the truth that God alone can do so. Only Jesus can bridge the gap between God and man created by our own sin, thus bringing us back into communication with God.

If Satan, therefore, can deceive people into thinking that this spiritual dimension can be satisfied in other ways, he will succeed in keeping people's eyes closed to the truth. For many people the pursuit of selfish objectives (as opposed to God's plan for their lives) is sufficient to keep them in rebellion against God. Satan deceives others, however, through involvement in what is known as 'the occult world'. *The occult* is an all-inclusive word used to describe the false spiritual pathways along which Satan takes people away from God.

There are many different pathways that Satan uses, such as astrology, transcendental meditation, spiritualism and ouija boards. Satan deludes people into believing that their particular aspect of the occult world is good and can be trusted. There is *no part* of the occult world that is good and none of it can be trusted – it is all built on the deceitful lies of Satan and if you pursue any area of occultism you are heading for spiritual disaster.

God's very first commandment says simply, 'You shall worship no other gods but me'. All occultism is a form of idolatory (false worship) irrespective of how superficial you may think it to be.

For example, spiritualism (by whatever name it is called) is specifically forbidden in the scriptures and all alleged contacts with dead people are Satanic deceptions by evil spirits. The temporary comfort people sometimes find in these experiences is used by Satan to detract from the very real comfort that God, by His presence, wants to bring into their lives.

Even something as apparently innocuous as horoscopes is part of the occult world. When people start to look for that 'exciting contact which will lead to new experiences' or for the 'unexpected telephone call which will bring difficult times ahead' they are allowing false predictions to give their lives direction. They are submitting to a power which is not of God. God would have us look to Him for guidance and trust Him for our future. Other occult practices which come into the same sort of category are visits to fortune tellers, gypsy palm readers, the use of tarot cards, reading tea leaves, letting superstitious practices control what we do, etc., etc.

The occult world is real – it is also dangerous. And if at the present time you have (or have ever had) any involvement whatsoever in any of its many forms confess it to God, renounce it and leave it behind you once and for all. This may mean that you will have to burn any objects, books or charms etc., which you previously enjoyed or valued (an account of an event such as this in New Testament times is given in Acts 19 vs. 11–20). Until you do this your Christian life will not grow and mature, you will not learn to trust the living God in all the circumstances of your life and God will not be able to bless and use you in the way He wants to.

Sometimes people need a lot of help in sorting out their own situations. If you have problems which you think may arise from occult activity with which you need help, seek out a mature Christian, preferably someone with experience of counselling people in this area. If the minister of your church is not able to help directly he is almost certain to know of someone who can.

The things that we have looked at in this chapter are just some of the areas of our lives where a Christian commitment will have an effect on the way we live. They are only examples of the sort of issues you will have to face. Your circumstances are special for you and the issues involved will probably be completely different, but do not think that your problems are so special that God will make a moral exception for you.

It isn't easy, I know that. And Paul himself told his readers to, 'work out their own salvation with fear and trembling'. This does not mean that we can work out for ourselves a way of salvation independent of the provision that God has made for us in Christ, but that we must work out the consequences of our salvation in the world in which God has placed us to live. It *is* great to be a Christian but the consequences of living the Christian life in a world which does not readily accept the Lordship of Christ will always be difficult.

God *will* give you the strength to cope. He *will* sustain you in difficult moments. He *will* honour you for the stand you make for Him. Life is for living and the only life worth living is the one with Jesus in control.

Chapter 3

Time for God

Personal Devotions: Guidelines
for Joy and Growth

'Personal devotions' is simply a phrase that describes the daily routines through which Christians maintain their relationship with God. They *are* important and there are some *guidelines* that will help you with getting them established in your own Christian life. But note that I have used the word *guidelines* and not *rules*. For there are almost as many effective routines as there are Christians. And if I were to say 'this is what you must do every day' it may well be wise and sensible advice for some Christians, but for a large number it would be impractical and inappropriate and they might fall into the trap of thinking that because they can't keep up with the 'rules' it is impossible for them to live the Christian life and they might as well give up now! Therein lies the danger of setting rules about things which are personal.

In Jesus's day the Pharisees (Jewish religious leaders) were very keen on making every minute detail of personal devotion and religious practice into a strict rule and Jesus condemned them for completely missing the boat of religious understanding. We must be careful, therefore, not to impose on other people what is important to us but which is not a requirement of scripture.

There *are* things for which rules are absolutely vital – in the realm of moral behaviour for example. But these things must be restricted to those areas which God Himself has made the subject of laws in the scriptures.

What Did Jesus Do?
When you read the gospels you will find that there were two major constituents of Jesus's personal devotional life which He used to maintain His daily relationship with God the Father. They were prayer and reading the scriptures. These same elements, therefore, are the ones which will be important to us. It seems that there were three aspects to prayer in Jesus's life:

(*a*) *times of being alone with God* for a regular, extended time of prayer – often before dawn. This was specially important to Him when He faced major decisions or events in His life (such as choosing the disciples and just before His crucifixion).

(*b*) *the continuous 'conversation' with God* during the daily activities of His life and ministry – He would be constantly talking to God about what was happening around Him and listening to God's response. So, prayer is not just talking to God, it is also listening to God speaking to us.

(*c*) *meeting together* for prayer with other Jews at the regular synagogue meetings. This is just one aspect of the synagogue worship that Jesus was used to. The direct comparison for Christians today is meeting together for prayer in the fellowship of the local church – this is so important that a separate chapter has been devoted to the subject of church life.

What guidelines for our personal devotional life can we learn from these things which were important to Jesus and from teaching contained in other parts of the Bible?

Firstly, that if it was necessary for Jesus, the Son of God

(who never sinned) to spend time alone in prayer with His Father, how much more necessary must it be for us (whose lives are constantly affected by the consequences of sin) to make similar provision.

Guideline Number One: Make time to be alone with God in prayer

Don't worry if you have no idea yet as to what you would do in such a time – even if it was only to be five minutes! Just make up your mind here and now that time alone with God is important and decide what time of the day would be most suitable for you.

Some people prefer to get up early. Others are able to use their lunch hour effectively. Others prefer the evening. Mothers with children to get off to school often take time off with God after the family have departed for the day. When, doesn't matter. Whether or not you do make time for prayer does matter.

Whenever it is that you have this time alone with God, I strongly recommend that you also get into the discipline of always beginning and ending each day with God. At the beginning – maybe even before you get out of bed, thank the Lord for a new day, tell Him you love Him, that you want to be obedient to His promptings and that you need His strength to cope with the many responsibilities, pressures and temptations that you are going to face. After all, your life now belongs to Him so it is the most logical thing possible to commit your day to Him.

Then, at the end of the day look back at all that has happened. Ask God to remind you of any sins that you have committed, so that you can confess them and ask for forgiveness; thank the Lord for any special blessings or answers to prayer that you have encountered; pray for anyone who God has used you to help, talk to about Himself or simply made you concerned about during the day; ask the Lord for wisdom on how to cope with any major problems you face; then ask His Holy Spirit to fill your mind with His peace as you go to sleep. That may sound a lot, but it needn't take longer than a few minutes and it will add immeasurably to the quality and power of your Christian life.

Guideline Number Two: Begin and end each day with prayer

Returning now to that longer time you are going to spend alone with God, whenever it is or however long it may be, the key question is, 'How are you going to fill the time?'

To help us answer this, remember how important the Old Testament was to Jesus in His life and ministry. He knew the scriptures very well. Indeed, when He faced temptation in the wilderness He used quotations from the Bible to confront Satan's attacks. He quoted from prophecy regularly and much of His teaching was simply an extension of all that God had already said to the Jewish people over many hundreds of years. Not only did He know the scriptures, He used them.

Jesus knew that the scriptures were (and still are) the very Word of God himself and that the devil has no power when faced with scriptural truths. God's word is also described as: (a) a *mirror* – to show us our own condition and needs so that we will constantly turn to God for His help; (b) *bread* – to feed our spiritual growth and (c) a *light* – to show us the way ahead. It is therefore necessary for us as Christians to know and apply the scriptures in our own lives.

Our Bible is divided into two sections. The Old Testament contains: the history of God's dealing with man in general and the Jewish people in particular; prophecy, which includes the foretelling of coming events (many of which have already been fulfilled) and the proclaiming of God's word to His people; poetry and wisdom written as an expression of man's experience with God. These are the books which Jesus read and used.

We also have the New Testament which contains: the Gospels which tell us about Jesus's life, death and resurrection; the Acts of the Apostles which describe the history of the early church; the letters to Christian communities that were established in the first century; and the amazing Revelation given by God to the Apostle John about the future history of the world.

Guideline Number Three: Always read the Bible during your time alone with God

The Bible is a big book and many people find the idea of reading it right through pretty formidable. Fortunately, there are many different types of Bible reading aids available to help you. Most of them suggest you read just a small section of the Bible each day (sometimes only one or two verses) and then provide you with some helpful explanatory notes about what you have read. In this way you will learn a lot about key parts of the Bible in a fairly short period of time. Some of these reading plans also provide a special introductory course for new Christians. Your local Christian bookshop will show you all the different types of Bible reading helps that you can get and advise you as to the best one to suit you.

If you enjoy reading you will also enjoy and benefit from reading longer sections of the Bible from time to time. Choose one of the Gospels (Mark or Luke are good to start with), or if you prefer the Old Testament have a go at some of the adventures of the Children of Israel recorded in the book of Joshua. When you have read a chapter put a small tick at the end of the last verse to remind you of what you have read. You'll be surprised at how quickly you will read much of the Bible.

As you read you will find that the Holy Spirit draws your special attention to things which are of importance *to you*. It's helpful to keep a pencil or fine ball-point pen ready so that you can underline these verses and make some notes in the margin. This will both help you to learn important lessons and be a useful reminder in the future.

You should also try learning these special verses off by heart so that you can think about them at any time. You may well be in a situation occasionally when you don't have access to a Bible and you will find it invaluable to remember passages of scripture which mean a lot to you. The more you learn of the Bible the more resources you will have available to live the Christian life.

There are many different translations of the Bible available. If you are using a Bible that was given to you in childhood it is quite likely to be the Authorized Version. Whilst this is a very beautiful translation, it is also 16th Century English and very hard to understand, so I strongly recommend that you get yourself a Bible in modern English. The two versions most easy to use and understand are the Good News Bible and the New International Version. Either of these would be ideal.

Whether you are going to read just a few verses or several chapters, always pray before you read. Choose your own words but try and include the various ideas mentioned in the following sample prayer:

> 'Thank you Lord that the Bible is a living book
> through which you speak to people today. Help me
> to understand what I read so that I will learn more
> about You and more about how You want me to
> live day by day.'

After reading your Bible, now is the time to pray. Whilst set prayers can be helpful, remember that this is a time when you are talking to your Heavenly Father. He wants to hear *you*, the real you, talking, and not just you repeating someone else's prayer. Prayer doesn't have to be lengthy or complicated to be effective. You matter to God, your life has a purpose, and the more natural and honest you are in talking with Him, the easier you will find it to be open to all that He wants to do in and through your life.

Guideline Number Four: Use your Bible reading as a starting point for prayer. But don't let your starting point also be the finishing point!

A good place to start in prayer is with the passage of scripture you have been reading. You may have understood something special for the first time – thank God for it. You may have realised that in some area of your life you've been dishonest, selfish, or unkind – tell Him you're sorry and ask for forgiveness. You may have been challenged to let God have more say in the way you live – tell Him that that is what you want and ask Him to give you the strength to go through with it. Whatever it is, you will find there are many ways in which God speaks to us through the Bible and if you start your prayer time with thoughts based on your reading you will never run out of ideas.

In addition to the aspects of Jesus's prayer life that we looked at earlier, Jesus also prayed with His disciples and taught them about prayer. The disciples had just the same problems as we have when it comes to knowing how to pray. One day they came to Jesus and said, 'Lord, teach us how to pray'. Jesus then showed them a pattern for prayer which we call The Lord's Prayer or The Family Prayer.

Earlier Jesus had been explaining to the disciples how the Pharisees weren't going to get very far in prayer just by repeating set prayers over and over again. That certainly wasn't the way to talk to your Father! Unfortunately, the Christian church has made The Lord's Prayer into just that sort of prayer and instead of using the ideas it contains as a pattern for all our praying, we tend to repeat The Lord's Prayer at every opportunity. It is in danger of becoming the meaningless repetition that Jesus condemned!

If we use The Lord's Prayer as Jesus intended, however, it can become for us a very simple and precious pattern for our major times of prayer – a pattern that is capable of almost infinite extension as we grow and mature as Christians.

Guideline Number Five: Use The Lord's Prayer as a pattern for prayer (not as a prayer that must be repeated without effort or thought).

Let's have a look at the pattern Jesus gave us. The first two lines, in the version that most people will know, are:

> 'Our Father, who art in heaven,
> Hallowed be Thy name.'

These opening lines are a recognition that God is Lord of heaven and earth and that He cares for us in a spiritual way as the very best of human fathers should care for his children, even though His eternal home is in heaven. There are many precious things to be learned from realising how much God loves us and cares for us. From realising this it is only a short step to the idea of worshipping God. The word worship simply means 'offering to God that which is worthwhile'. At this point in our prayer, therefore, we can offer ourselves to God afresh for each day. Perhaps, too, as we remember that His name is special we'll be reminded that we shouldn't use it as an expletive in conversation. When we hear other people swearing in this way we should begin to understand something of the hurt that God must feel when people, who do not love Him, use His name to decorate their conversation.

> 'Thy Kingdom come, Thy will be done,
> On earth as it is in heaven.'

This part of the prayer is both a deliberate act of

submission to the will of God and a positive prayer that God's people will be obedient to His purposes. So, in our prayer for people and situations the most positive prayer we can pray is that the individuals involved will be open to, and obedient to, the will of God.

Prayer is powerful, and even those who do not recognise God as their Father or Jesus as their Saviour can, by the power of prayer, be encouraged to change their minds, their motives and even their plans as they are challenged by the Holy Spirit. So, submission to the will of God is not a negative thing at all. It is, very positively, working hand-in-hand with God.

There are many ways of interpreting the phrase, 'Thy Kingdom come'. But, basically, I believe we can look at the rest of Jesus's teaching and say that when He talked about the Kingdom of God He was referring to three particular things:

1. In the whole of Jesus's ministry He was very concerned that *God should be active in the lives of individuals*. When people receive Jesus as Lord the Kingdom of God has really come into their lives. So when we pray 'Thy Kingdom come' it is an ideal opportunity to pray for our friends who are not yet Christians, but whom God is encouraging us to pray for.
2. *The rule of God on earth*. One day Jesus *is* going to come again. And the Kingdom of God will be established throughout the world. Jesus talked a lot about this to His disciples and His conversations are recorded in the Gospels.
3. The third way in which Jesus referred to the Kingdom of God is illustrated in many of the parables and refers to *God's people living Godly lives*. In Chapter Seven we will spend quite a long time looking at how one of the Holy Spirit's responsibilities is to produce in us the characteristics of God Himself. When we let Him do this the Kingdom of God has come into both our lives and the lives of every single person who is

touched by the way we live for Him. So here we can pray for understanding as to how we should react to the known events of the day in a way that is honouring to God, and for wisdom to respond wisely in all the situations that we cannot anticipate!

'Give us this day our daily bread'.

At this point in the prayer our attention is turned from the needs of others to our own personal needs. The phrase 'daily bread' *does* refer to our basic food requirements, but it can also include other personal needs which we are aware of. So now is the opportunity to bring to God all those personal matters that are concerning us.

'And forgive us our trespasses
As we forgive those who trespass against us.'

The word trespasses is an old word which means sins – the things that we do wrong. They are the things for which we all need to be forgiven. On this question of forgiveness, however, The Lord's Prayer is very challenging. For the phrase, 'forgive us our trespasses' is linked with the next phrase, 'as we forgive those who trespass against us'. The implication is that unless we are willing to extend to other people the sort of forgiveness that we are asking of God, then we are not able to receive the forgiveness that God longs to give us! So now is an opportunity to be quiet and think if there are any people who have hurt us, whom we need to forgive, before we can ask God to forgive us for the things we've done wrong. If there are any, then we need to tell God that we want to forgive them and be determined that as soon as possible after our prayer time is over we will go out of our way to put that forgiveness into practice. For example, it may be necessary to go and say sorry to someone we have offended. We can then, with a clear conscience, review our own lives before God and ask Him to draw our attention to anything which He's concerned

44

about so that we may be able to confess it and receive His forgiveness.

> 'And lead us not into temptation,
> But deliver us from evil.'

The words of a current Christian song refer to Jesus in this way: 'He's my rock, He's my fortress, He's my deliverer, in Him do I trust.' Jesus really is the only one who can deliver us from the powers of evil. For it was He who defeated Satan on the cross of Calvary, and whilst the devil will continue to try and deceive us into thinking that it is he (not Jesus) who is all powerful, when we take authority over him in the name of Jesus we stand against him in the name of the Great Deliverer. So we can, in the words of The Lord's Prayer, come to Jesus absolutely confident that He is the one who is able to deliver us from evil and from all the forces of darkness that would seek to disturb us and to distress us as we live our Christian lives.

The phrase 'lead us not into temptation' is translated in more modern versions of The Lord's Prayer as 'do not bring us to the test' or 'do not bring us through hard testing'. There is no way in which God can tempt us to do wrong and we have, therefore, in this prayer the desire expressed to God that He will not test us beyond the limits of our faith. The more secure our faith in Jesus is, the more extensive these limits are. God is always encouraging us to live our lives at a deeper level of trust and active faith, but if we are not prepared to be obedient then it may well be necessary for Him to put us through various situations which will indeed test us and enable us to find out how reliable He is in the midst of crisis. God *is* to be trusted and He will not test us beyond that which we can bear when we place ourselves in His hands.

> 'For Thine is the Kingdom, the power and the
> glory, For ever and ever, Amen.'

This final phrase of The Lord's Prayer does not appear

in the Bible at all. It was added by the church as a means of incorporating the pattern of prayer, which Jesus gave to His disciples, into the set prayers used in public worship. The words used are an acknowledgement that all power and glory belong to God both now and throughout the whole of eternity. The word *Amen* means that you agree with all that's gone before.

As you experiment in your prayer times you will find that they become more important to you, but don't make the mistake of thinking that you can only pray to God during your special time of prayer! We mentioned earlier that Jesus was constantly in touch with His Father, and so can we be. Whatever the time of day, or situation in which you are involved, pray briefly in your mind to God for help, for wisdom, for guidance, for patience, for kindness, for anything which you need and for which you must depend on Him.

One of the most effective ways of building up your faith is to see your prayers being answered. Unfortunately our memories are so short that unless the situations are dramatic we are not very good at remembering what we have prayed about!

Guideline Number Six: Keep a record of the major things God leads you to pray about and record your answers.

I, personally, have found it very encouraging to keep a regular prayer diary. This is simply a day-by-day list of the main things that I am led to pray about. It's easy then to look back and see what God has done in response to prayer. Use your experiences to build up your faith and be encouraged to launch out to achieve even greater things for God.

Chapter 4

You and the Church

Life in the Local Fellowship
of Christians

When you became a Christian you became a member of THE Church. You may already have been attending a local 'church', but if not it is important that you do join a group of local Christians for worship, fellowship and practical Christian ministry as soon as possible.

First, however, it is important to understand a little about what the church really is. The very word 'church' is confusing. We talk vaguely about 'going to church'. We hear opinions expressed by 'the church' on radio or television. And most Christians are members of a denomination with a title incorporating the word 'church', (e.g. United Reformed Church, Methodist Church, Church of England). Clearly, the word 'church' means different things at different times to different people. Originally, however, there was only one meaning of the word 'church' and it is important, therefore, that we understand what the Bible means when it uses the word 'church', and what the consequences are for us today.

When Paul used the word 'church' (or, rather, 'ecclesia', the Greek word used for 'church') he was referring to a group of people who believed in Jesus and who met together for worship and practical Christian ministry. The actual word he used simply means an assembly of people who are called by God. He referred to this group of people as the Body of Christ. He used this phrase because they were continuing the ministry of Jesus and fulfilling Jesus' prophecy that they would actually do (with their bodies) the same sort of things that Jesus had done whilst on earth.

Jesus ministered to other people through His body. When He spoke to them He used His mind, mouth and lips. When He healed them He would often reach out His hand and touch them. When He went to visit people He would use His legs to get there.

The local church today, therefore, is not primarily a building or a denomination but simply the Body of Christ at work in the community. Just as a human body has many different parts (or members), all dependent one on the other, so the church has many different members who (should) work together so that the overall will of the head of the body (that is, Christ) is fulfilled.

As the early church developed it gradually acquired:

(*a*) *Creeds* – fundamental beliefs embraced by a group of Christians, originally established so as to eliminate heresy;

(*b*) *Doctrines* – teaching by which the Christian faith is applied, both individually and to the Body of Christ as a fellowship and in its relationship with the world; and

(*c*) *Structures* – the way the church is organised and run on a local, national and international scale.

Unfortunately, whilst most Christians agree on the principal contents of their various creeds, not all agree about doctrines and structures. As a result there are denominations. The Body of Christ is therefore divided by denominationalism – and usually there are several different groups of Christians meeting separately in the same locality.

48

No *one* denomination can claim to be 'THE Church'. It is only *one* of many ways in which Christians are organised into a structural relationship with particular theological emphases (see Appendix B for brief summaries of the principal distinguishing features of the major denominations).

If challenged, the majority of Christians would find it hard to justify their allegiance to a particular denomination. Most are members of a certain denomination for circumstantial (as opposed to doctrinal) reasons, e.g.

(a)   their parents went there,
(b)   it is close to home,
(c)   they have friends who go there,
(d)   they were converted through its influence.

As church fellowships grew most decided that they wanted a special building in which to meet. These church buildings have been a mixed blessing. For the buildings in which we meet for worship are not *the* church. Groups of Christians were called a church long before they had special buildings in which to worship God. Our use of the same word to describe the building as we use to describe the fellowship of Christians has led to considerable confusion.

It is clearly physically impossible, therefore, for a group of believers (who *are* the church) to actually 'go to church' – they can only go to the building in which the church meets for worship. Whilst it is important that the building Christians use should be adequate for their purpose and honouring to God, pre-occupation with buildings has become one of the major obstacles to the renewal and growth of the twentieth century church.

To summarise, therefore, the church is the Body of Christ at work in today's world. It is made up of individuals who are personally committed to Jesus Christ as Lord and who share together in a common fellowship. Its object is to continue the work of Christ and in particular to be obedient to Jesus' final words of instruction to preach the message about repentence and forgiveness of sin (Luke 24:47) to all nations.

Joining the Church
If you are a new Christian and not yet worshipping regularly with a local congregation, I would strongly advise you to attend the nearest local church (irrespective of denomination) which has as many of the following features as possible:

1. A minister (or leader if there is no resident minister) who is: encouraged by the fact that you have become a Christian; is concerned to help new Christians grow in their faith; accepts the Bible as the Word of God and gives good teaching from it.
2. Small group fellowship meetings (sometimes called house-groups) which meet on a mid-week night as well as Sunday services – especially if there is a special one for new Christians.
3. A regular church prayer meeting.
4. Members who are not only warm towards each other but also interested in building relationships with newcomers, and
5: Sunday Services which are relevant, interesting and alive.

You will, indeed, be fortunate if you find any church in your immediate locality which has *all* these character-istics! It is important that you feel at home in whichever congregation you decide to join so try a few before deciding which one you are going to attend regularly.

It is equally important, however, that, when you have decided which it is to be, you commit yourself to it wholeheartedly and become part of the life of the fellow-ship. You cannot benefit from all that the church has to offer if you flip from one congregation to another and never settle down with any of them. Nor will you be a help
50

to others who need your work and fellowship. As part of the Body of Christ you need to be integrated with other members.

Life in the Local Church

Attendance at church services is important, but this is only part of a Christian's overall involvement in the life of the church. There are seven ingredients that are essential for healthy life and growth – both individually, and together with other Christians:

(a)   worship,
(b)   praise,
(c)   teaching and preaching,
(d)   prayer,
(e)   fellowship
(f)   sacraments, and
(g)   service.

We will now consider each of these in turn.

(a) Worship. The word worship simply means 'offering to God that which is worthwhile and worthy of Him'. In the last chapter of the book we will see that 'true worship' (as defined by Paul) means giving to God the thing we value most – our life.

In common church language, however, the word worship is often mistakenly used just to describe the regular Sunday services. Whilst our services, which should allow for all the elements of church life listed above, are one way of expressing worship, they were never intended to be the totality of our worship. Many of the problems experienced by church fellowships arise because the *real meaning* of the word worship has not been appreciated by members of the congregation, and attendance at morning service is considered to be the *only* element of worship. It is the giving of our time (which is precious) and ourselves (as a result of God's dealings with us during the service) that, more accurately, expresses the spirit of true worship.

We worship God with our bodies, therefore, whenever we give of our time or our abilities. We worship Him with our resources whenever we give materially to any cause, organisation or individual as a practical outworking of our faith. We worship Him with our minds whenever we submit ourselves to the authority of God's word, either written in the scripture, or ministered directly to us by the Holy Spirit. We worship Him with our lips whenever we open our mouths to praise His name or let them be used in His service.

(b) Praise. In the Psalms we read that God dwells in the praises of His people. A praising people is therefore going to be very aware of God's presence and power. When we thank God for who He is, we are praising Him; when we tell Him we love Him we are praising Him, and when in our hearts we rejoice because of Jesus we are praising Him.

We can express such praise in silence, in conversation, in prayer, or much more commonly, with our lips as we sing in company with other Christians. Thanksgiving is closely related to praise and is usually associated with thanking God for what He gives to us. Both praise and thanksgiving are important elements of worship.

Later on in this book we will see how a Christian can be at peace, even when circumstances all around him are far from peaceful. In a similar way it is quite natural for a Christian to be able to continue praising in the middle of circumstances which, humanly speaking, have nothing attractive about them, for our praise is directed towards God who never changes.

When we praise God something happens to us inside. We become more alert to the presence of the Holy Spirit; we become more willing to listen and be obedient to what God may be saying to us; and we become more conscious of the needs of others. A praising people is a powerful people.

(c) Teaching and Preaching. There are two keys to the art of good teaching. The first is a teacher with the gift of communication and the second is a pupil who is willing to learn. Christians are not exempt from this fact of life. A good church, therefore, will be wise in its choice of teachers, both for the Sunday School and the adult congregation. A bad teacher (or preacher for that matter) can have the effect of killing off any interest in an otherwise willing congregation. A good teacher will so teach the congregation that they will hardly be aware of the fact that they are being taught!

As members of a congregation it is important that we should be willing to learn and also be patient with the teachers who have the responsibility to interpret the Bible to us. Pray that their ministry will be effective. The most important thing we need to learn about is the content of the Bible. For the Bible contains the very Word of God. It is a living book because its writing was inspired by the living Holy Spirit and the same Holy Spirit interprets it to us now to meet our present-day needs. It is always, therefore, up-to-date.

The Bible contains all that we need to know about God and how we should live. When Paul was writing to the young man Timothy, he referred to the Old Testament as being 'useful for teaching truth, rebuking error, correcting faults and giving instruction for right living'. It still is – and we have the benefit of having the New Testament as well.

The best place for straightforward teaching to take place is at the mid-week Bible study or house-group – a place where you can ask questions and gain understanding in discussion. But all sermons that are preached at Sunday services will contain an element of teaching. So it is wise to have your Bible with you, so that you can mark carefully anything you learn which is particularly relevant or important.

Whilst teaching is a very important part of preaching, the main purpose of preaching is to invoke a response and not just give information, however important that information may be. When Peter preached that first sermon, on the day God gave His Holy Spirit to the church, the people there were taught the truth about Jesus. But they were also convicted in their hearts and responded to what had been preached by becoming Christians. So God will often use preaching to convict people of sin that they may be converted.

At other times people will be encouraged, challenged, humbled, convinced, and experience various other reactions as the Holy Spirit takes the words that are preached and interprets them to the minds of individuals in the congregation. The same sermon will often have very different effects on different people!

Preaching and teaching are very important aspects of church life. The sermon is not the time for sleeping (!) but for listening, prayerfully, to what God has to say to us so that the church may be built up in the faith and be an effective communicator of the gospel to the world outside.

(d) *Prayer*. Prayer, at its simplest, is talking with God. In the chapter on Personal Devotions we saw the importance and value of personal prayer. But Jesus also prayed with His disciples and, in fellowship with others, at the synagogue. Prayer, therefore, should be an integral part of our church life as well.

Formal prayers are always part of church services, and in some fellowships there is also the opportunity for individuals to participate in prayer, either silently or out loud. Most also make provision in the prayers of intercession (when we are praying to God on behalf of other people), to pray about major concerns within the lives of members of the congregation.

In the Acts of the Apostles we read that the early church spent its time 'learning from the apostles, taking part in the fellowship,' sharing in the fellowship meals (our communion services are equivalent to these) and in prayer'. It would appear that meetings for prayer were a major part of
54

their fellowship life. If a church fellowship is to fulfil its responsibilities, as the Body of Christ, in the local community then it must be praying together for that community and for the effect of the church upon it. It is also through prayer that God so changes the life of a church that its local ministry becomes effective.

A good pattern for church prayer is one which allows for the benefits of both small prayer groups and larger meetings of the whole fellowship. This is easily arranged by having small group meetings (house-groups) one week and a general prayer meeting of the whole church the following week, and so on, alternately.

You will learn a lot through sharing in prayer with your fellow-Christians. There is no need to feel that because you are a new Christian you are not experienced enough to pray. The honesty of your prayer is more important to God than the way you express it.

(e) Fellowship. Fellowship is more than friendship. For it is possible to have fellowship in Christ with someone you don't particularly like at a human level. Fellowship is enjoying and benefiting from the company of others because they are Christians – people who have trusted Jesus to be their Saviour and worship Him as Lord.

Christians, therefore, have a bond between them which is far deeper than any human friendship can ever be. They share the same Heavenly Father and so, far more than being friends, are, literally, brothers and sisters in Christ.

It is important to maintain our fellowship with other Christians in our local church. We do that by sharing with them in the work and ministry of the church; by honestly discussing and praying about any real differences that may arise between us; by encouraging each other to use the gifts and abilities that God has given us; by providing for the material needs of others; by welcoming and caring for strangers who may come into our church services; and in a host of other ways which will become relevant as the Christian life is lived in the fellowship of the local church.

Mid-week house-groups which meet together for Bible study, prayer, discussion and encouragement are a vital part of the life of a fellowship. It is often through these that we can make very deep and lifelong friendships on which we can depend in times of difficulty and through which God often leads and encourages us into new areas of service. Fellowship is a very special Christian experience – without fellowship our faith is unlikely to grow and we will miss out on many of the blessings which God waits to give to His children.

(*f*) *Sacraments*. A sacrament is a special aspect of the church's ministry. Different denominations recognise different things as 'sacraments' (such as baptism, confirmation, marriage, communion, etc.) but most agree that Holy Communion and Baptism are the key ones.

Some churches call the communion service 'the Breaking of Bread', others 'the Sacrament of the Lord's Supper', others 'the Eucharist', and others, simply, 'Communion'. Whatever the sacrament is called the form of service follows the pattern which Jesus gave to His disciples at their last meal together on the night before He was crucified. He broke a piece of bread and said, 'This is My body which is given for you, do this in memory of Me'. And then He took the cup of wine and said, 'This cup is God's New Covenant sealed with My blood, which is poured out for you'. The bread and the wine therefore represent the body and the blood of Jesus Christ and when, in fellowship with other Christians, we receive the bread and the wine we are not only remembering the death of Jesus but also worshipping God as we thank Him for sending Jesus to die in our place on the cross.

For many people the service of Holy Communion is central to their personal experience of God for in it they are constantly made aware of God's love, the sacrifice of Jesus and the only reasonable response that we can make – the giving of ourselves to God.

The other sacrament which most of the churches

recognise is Baptism. Symbolically this represents the death and burial of one's old self and the rising again to new life in Christ. This image is most accurately portrayed in the ceremony of Believers' Baptism which involves going down beneath the water (for a moment!) and rising again to live for God, having totally identified oneself with Christ. The sacrament of Baptism was instituted in obedience to Jesus' command to 'Baptise disciples in the name of the Father, the Son and the Holy Spirit'.

Many of the churches carry out a baptismal ceremony on infant children, the significance of which is only completely fulfilled at a second ceremony when the child is old enough to decide for himself or herself that he or she wishes to continue with their Christian faith. In the Anglican and Roman Catholic churches, for example, this is known as Confirmation.

(g) Service. Christianity is not a passive religion. Much of Jesus' teaching was designed to show people that serving others is of greater importance than serving ourselves. There are many different ways in which we can serve both God and our fellow-man in the life of the church. In a Christian fellowship everyone is of equal importance before God and provided we are fulfilling the service to which God has called us – whether that is to clean the pews or be ordained as a minister – then it should be done to the very best of our ability and to the glory of God.

In addition to the many functions within the life of a fellowship which provide avenues of service for members, it is absolutely vital that every local church should also be alert to the potential of serving God in the community outside. Serving God in the community is a necessary consequence of our commitment to Christ. By example, and in His parables, Jesus underlined the responsibility we have to God to express our love for Him by loving and serving others.

Such service may be active evangelism amongst those

who are not Christians, providing for the material needs of the elderly, running a play group for the children of young mothers, visiting the sick, sharing belongings, work on school Parent/Teacher Associations, and even involvement in local politics. Whatever it is that God calls *you* to do, always remember that the *way* you do it is a witness to others of the faith that you have.

Chapter 5

What is God Looking For in Me?

Growing the Fruit of the Spirit

One of the first questions new Christians often ask is 'What must I do now?' They believe, and quite rightly, that God is interested in the way that they live and relate to other people. They know there are elements in their own lives of which they are ashamed and which are going to have to change, and they don't want to make a mess of their first stumbling efforts at being a living witness for Jesus Christ. To put it in a nutshell, they don't want to put a foot wrong, or, in religious language, they don't want to sin.

Some Christians, who are a little older in the faith, also have problems in this area. They, too, have set out to live as they thought God would want them to. But time and time again they have been caught in a trap as they have failed to live up to their own standards, and are now beginning to despair of ever being able to live like a 'proper Christian'!

Others, often much older Christians, have settled for a status quo in which they know that Jesus is the truth and that the basic teaching of Christianity is right. But they also know themselves and the limits they feel able to go in being obedient to the Lord, and they have settled for living out their lives in a gentle compromise between the will of God and the strength of man, believing they are doing their best and can do no more. The real challenge of moving out into new territory for God has not been appreciated.

The medicine for each of these three conditions is the same: (a) understanding sin, and (b) realising that it is the Holy Spirit's responsibility to both show us how to live day-by-day and give us the power to be able to do it!

The simplest definition of sin is disobedience. Not merely disobedience with respect to a list of negative commandments – we cannot be obedient to God's will for our lives and break His laws at the same time – but disobedience to the moment-by-moment prompting of God's Holy Spirit. It is obedience to His leading that results in the characteristics of God's Holy Spirit becoming obvious in our lives. These characteristics are sometimes called the fruit of the Spirit. (See Gal. 5:22.)

They are all characteristics which are developed in the life of any Christian as a result of the Holy Spirit's active presence. No one can claim any of them by virtue of wealth, birth, personality, or education. Understanding this is absolutely vital – for otherwise one might be tempted to think that only highly intelligent or well-educated people, or those with attractive personalities, could live the Christian life. This would immediately exclude well over half the world's population! Jesus called people to Himself from all social and educational classes – there were no exceptions. So, as you read this chapter, don't feel that the things God is looking for in you are an impossible and, therefore, depressing target, but thank the Lord that He is going to achieve miracles in your life as you give the Holy Spirit freedom to get to work!

Paul made a list of these characteristics when he was writing to the Galatian Christians. The order in which he listed them is significant. Love is a language that all can understand irrespective of who they are or where they live. It is not surprising, therefore, to find that the first fruit of the Holy Spirit's presence is *Love*.

Love

Love is being more concerned for the welfare of others than for one's own interests. Such love was supremely expressed by Jesus who, on the cross, took upon Himself the sinfulness of man so that redeemed people could enjoy a living relationship with a holy God. Love, however, is not just providing for someone else's needs. Ensuring that someone else thinks well of us, because of what we do for them, is not love but an expression of pride, selfishness and self-interest. Many a marriage, for example, is held together by vested self-interest masquerading as love. Love is expressed by providing for the interests of someone else irrespective of what that person will think of us, or is able and willing to do for us.

God's Holy Spirit will prompt us to express real love in every area of our lives – for our families, our friends, our colleagues at work, for complete strangers and, of course, in our relationship with God Himself. It is, primarily, for this reason that the life of a new Christian is often so radically changed that others notice the difference. New Christians, therefore, are often the most effective witnesses to their faith. They have lots of non-Christian friends who will be curious to know what has happened!

The expression of love is sometimes costly – in terms of time, money, resources, ambition and, indeed, any of the values which the world considers important. But, there is no way that any Christian can enjoy the next fruit of God's Holy Spirit without being obedient to the voice of love.

Joy

Joy is a specially Christian quality. The word has a meaning which the world cannot match. It is not the same as happiness – although a joyful person is often a happy one. Joy is that special sort of Christian happiness which comes from being obedient to God's will. A wordly person may be happy because all the circumstances of his life are currently favourable and to his liking. A Christian may also be happy in such circumstances, but over and above any circumstantial happiness is a joy that is only present when the circumstances are within God's will.

No amount of circumstantial or materialistic happiness can ever make a Christian joyful, if, in his heart, he knows that a deliberate act of disobedience has contributed to his current circumstances and God would really have him somewhere else and doing something else with his life.

The opposite of this can also be true. A Christian may well be in circumstances which, humanly speaking, would not normally be considered as happy. But, when those circumstances are a direct result of being obedient to the will of God then an inner joy becomes the predominant emotion, taking precedence over all the consequences of the immediate external circumstances.

Christians through the ages have testified to the joy brought into their lives when they submitted to God's will. Already we have mentioned 'God's will for our lives' on several occasions. So important is this subject that the last chapter of the book will be devoted completely to it.

Peace
In a Christian sense peace is much more than the absence of war. The often used phrase 'peace which passes all understanding' attempts to express the unique characteristic of Christian peace. Like joy, this peace can be experienced in the middle of apparently contrary circumstances. There are three aspects of Christian peace that need to be understood: Peace with God, Peace with our Fellow Human Beings, and Peace with Ourselves.

(a) Peace with God
It is only because Jesus paid for our sin on Calvary that it is possible for us to be at peace with God at all. The essence of that peace lies in confession (which means agreeing with God's verdict on our sinfulness), forgiveness (which God has promised to those who confess their sin – 1 John 1:9), and acceptance (of God's forgiveness by us, of us by God, and of ourselves as we are).

62

Most people have a mistaken idea of what confession is all about. The purpose and value of confession is rarely understood by new Christians because they only associate the meaning of the word with telling other people all the secrets of their lives.

It is only when we know a person really well that we are willing to take notice of anything they may say about us. The same applies to our relationship with God. If our relationship with Him is only distant, or even non-existent, then we can only communicate with God by repeating the well-worn phrases of set prayers. That is not to say that using set prayers, such as The General Confession, is not important – it is. But using such prayers must be a genuine expression of our feeling towards God and not a cover-up for an inadequate relationship with Him.

When something comes between a husband and wife who love each other very much, they don't need to tell each other that the relationship is broken – they know. In just the same way when we have damaged our relationship with God, we know, because we have lost some of our peace and joy.

Others may not notice this, at first that is, because we can be very clever at pretending to other people that our relationship with God is unbroken. But until we see our sin as God sees it and agree with His opinion of it, we cannot expect to be forgiven and regain our peace.

Before we knew God it was as if the sins we had committed were hard to notice against the grubby background of our lives. But when we first became Christians, God wiped the slate clean and gave us a fresh start, and even the smallest mark is now immediately obvious. Confession, therefore, is the vital first step towards keeping our relationship with God up-to-date.

Forgiveness is what we receive when we confess our sin to God. Forgiveness is received immediately – there is no time penalty to delay us from experiencing the love of God here and now. Our relationship with God is restored and we can carry on where we left off. God's forgiveness is total – His love has no limits and His peace can reign once more in our hearts. It is important to remember that God doesn't punish us for our sin – Jesus took that punishment on Himself when He died on the cross – although we may have to live with the consequences of our sin.

Then we must trust God and accept that He cannot deny His own words. He has said that those who confess *will* be forgiven. We must therefore trust this as fact and live in that forgiveness. The devil will try and deceive us into thinking that our sins are too great to be forgiven and that we are no longer acceptable to God. God's word says that 'even though our sins are as scarlet, they will be white as snow'. For God not to forgive those for whom Christ died would mean that Christ died in vain – He died, that you might be forgiven. Believe it, trust it, live it.

(b) Peace with our Fellow Human Beings

There were many people whom Jesus could have reacted against, but even on the cross He was able to say of His persecutors, 'Father, forgive them, they do not know what they are doing'.

Jesus recognised that in the great spiritual battle that culminated on Calvary the contestants were not the man Jesus and His captors, but God Himself and Satan. All His attackers were being used by the prince of darkness against the Son of God. So Jesus could, at one and the same time, hate the actions Satan encouraged people to bring against Him, and love the people whose spiritual eyes were so closed that they could not see how they were being manipulated.

We are encouraged in the scriptures to hate sin but, nevertheless, love those who sin – even if their sins are directed against us. If we desire to be obedient to God's word His Holy Spirit will give us the strength and desire to love people in this way. When people seem to be against you, therefore, you will still be able to love them even though you may hate, and be suffering for, the things they

64

are doing to you. That is the only way to be at peace with our fellow human beings, for otherwise we will let the hurts we have experienced in life be the source of bitterness, resentment and hate. Our spiritual lives will be poisoned and sometimes, even, we will suffer physically as a result of our failure to love, and express our love, by forgiveness. Medical evidence confirms that much mental and physical illness results from our failure to deal with these negative emotions. No wonder James said in his letter that we should confess our sins one to another that we may be *healed*.

To love others in this way requires the power of God. The Holy Spirit will give us that power – but the onus is on us to accept and apply that power in the face of a society which encourages people to act rather differently!

It takes two to have a disagreement. If you claim the power of the Holy Spirit you will be able to look at those who wrong you, and even persecute you, and see in them the person for whom Christ died. You will be able to love them even whilst hating the things they are doing and maintain your peace with your fellow human beings.

(c) Peace with Ourselves

Some people are able to confess their sins and accept God's forgiveness, but never seem to be able *to accept themselves*. The devil tells them that because they have sinned they are no good and that they had better opt out of this Christian thing and leave it to others.

If this is you, remember that Jesus only died for sinners. Therefore He died for you. He died so that you could have a new start to every single day of your life. There is no one whom God cannot use, but there are many people who are so ashamed of themselves that they don't give God the chance to even try.

Have the courage to trust what is clearly promised in the Bible. Begin every day holding God to His promises, thank Him for His love and go out into the day expecting Him to be at work in and through your life. He loves you just as you are, whatever you have done in the past and whatever your daily need may be.

You *are* special – don't let anyone deprive you of your authority to live the Christian life, or leave you with the impression that you are inferior in any way to others who may have different personalities from yours: God loves us all equally. You are a child of the King. He loves you and He cares for you as if you were the only person in the world. Let the Holy Spirit produce peace in your heart as you accept yourself in the way that God has already accepted you because of Jesus. Keep your relationship with Him fresh and up-to-date. He will never let you down.

Patience

Oak trees are strong. Oak trees grow very slowly. So don't be impatient with God if it seems as though He is moving very slowly in your life. He may be preparing you for some very special work which requires great spiritual strength. Believe that the Holy Spirit will give you the patience to accept (and even rejoice in) God's timing.

When we put ourselves in God's hands and let the Holy Spirit take over it is enough simply to wait upon God in every area of our lives and let Him direct us. Many Christians do get impatient, however, and are tempted not to trust God in particular areas of their lives. For example, with regard to marriage some seem to think that they know better than God Himself and as a result finish up marrying the wrong person rather than waiting for God's timing and choice.

If we really have let God have His way with our lives we can trust that He knows what is best for us with regard to marriage, our careers, our relationships, our time and every single area of our life that we can think of.

The word patience involves more, however, than our relationship with God. It also involves our relationships with other people. The spiritual life of many churches is often spoiled by the lack of patience shown by their

66

members with each other. Outsiders notice these things and when from time to time they may be challenged to think more deeply about Christian truth, they sub-consciously remind themselves that they have enough problems of their own without wanting to add to them by getting involved in the local church disputes! The effec-tiveness of our witness to others is often impaired by our attitudes.

On the other hand if, in all your relationships, you demonstrate the fruit of patience you will be surprised at how much easier it is to get on with people, and at the way those things which cause you to be impatient become less important.

Kindness and Goodness
These two fruits are very different, even though they may seem the same. Goodness is another way of saying Godli-ness. It is not surprising that God's Holy Spirit will produce in us the characteristics of God Himself. Good-ness is a personal characteristic embracing a quality of life, moral behaviour and personal thought patterns which are wholly good. Paul summarised this quality by listing the sort of thoughts (and consequential activities) that a Godly person would be interested in (Philippians 4:8) – things that are good, that deserve praise, things that are true, noble, right, pure, lovely and honourable.

In other places Paul lists all the evil things that are an expression of the sin within our lives. These are the things that we 'naturally' prefer to do. It is, therefore, a 'supernatural' work of God's Holy Spirit to give us a genuine desire for the things of God.

A good person will also be kind. But the quality of kindness requires the involvement of a third party; God, you *and* someone else. A kind person will act thoughtfully, generously, unselfishly and practically in the best interests of others. Kindness may include an element of self-sacrifice in terms of time, money or resources. The Good Samaritan, for example, was kind in that he considered the injured man's interests ahead of his own. Firstly, he stopped to help a Jew (someone all his social training would have told him to ignore). Then he put himself at risk from a similar attack by putting the injured man on his donkey and walking him slowly back to the nearest inn. Finally he gave money to the inn-keeper to pay for his care.

There are many opportunities for a Christian to show such practical kindness. All we have to do is to ask God to show them to us and then listen to that prompting voice of His Holy Spirit. There are many people who were converted to Christ because of the patient kindness of a Christian person which prompted them to ask, 'Why should someone else care about me?'

Faithfulness
Faithfulness is different from faith. It took a step of faith to hand your life back to God and trust Jesus as your Saviour. But to maintain that faith through the thick and thin of life is being faithful to the God who has called you to Himself. Faithfulness, to God, therefore, could be described as spiritual loyalty, especially during the circumstances in your life when you may be tempted to wonder what is happening to you, when the going is tough and people seem to be against you. To maintain your faith through all this is an act of faithfulness.

If we only had our own human resources it would be very easy to turn against God and blame Him for these things. But God has called us to live in a real world and being a Christian does not exempt us from the normal pressures of life. But God has promised to be with us moment-by-moment, day-by-day and if we keep our eyes upon Him the Holy Spirit will produce in us that essential fruit of faithfulness.

So, God is not looking for Christians who are only happy to serve Him when everything in the garden is lovely, what He needs is people who will be faithful to Him and testify to His love throughout their lives
68

whatever their temporal external circumstances may be; people who will maintain a living and up-to-date witness to the saving power of Jesus Christ; people who will continue to love others, be joyful and maintain their peace with God and man, even as they are tested in the crucibles of life.

But there is another aspect of faithfulness which, without the Holy Spirit's presence and power, will be impossible to achieve. That is, faithfulness to other people – even when they let us down. Even though Peter denied Jesus three times, Jesus stuck by him and on the Day of Pentecost (when God gave the Holy Spirit to the church) it was Peter who preached that first sermon through which three thousand people were converted! What would have happened to Peter if Jesus had turned his back on him? Rejected, with a burden of guilt weighing him down, at the best he would have returned to his fishing and become a bitter, foul-mouthed and bad-tempered individual. At the worst he would have followed Judas to a suicide's grave.

But Jesus was faithful to Peter, even when his actions didn't deserve it. The Holy Spirit will help us to behave in the same way towards other people. But we must let Him have His way with us, and not resist His promptings to continue loving and caring for those whom we don't like (or who obviously don't like us) and those who let us down time and time again.

Humility

A humble person is not a weak person. He is strong. Strong because he does not have to behave in a way that bolsters up his pride. He is free to do what is right whatever the situation and irrespective of the way his actions will reflect on his own personal reputation. Jesus perfectly expressed the essence of humility by putting aside His rights as the Son of God because of His willingness to be obedient to the cross for you and me.

Pride is an insidious enemy which eats away within us.

Pride prevents us from agreeing with someone who is right, because, for other reasons, we may not wish to associate with them. Pride is often a source of friction within the life of a church fellowship. God is always doing something new and if our pride insists that the only way that God will be allowed to work in this place is by repeating the things that we did last year, before the war or even in the last century, then we could find ourselves not only opposing our friends in the fellowship, but God Himself.

Pride cannot be rooted out by your deciding to be humble. Pride can only be overcome by accepting the work of the Holy Spirit in our hearts and letting the spirit of humility take root instead. Also, remember that true humility is not expressed by your concealing the gifts that God has given you. That is a false humility which denies others the benefit of your God-given abilities.

Self-Control

The last of Paul's fruits of the Spirit is certainly not the least. For the last one expresses in a practical way the spiritual reality of all the others.

A Christian cannot excuse his behaviour by hiding behind the facade of 'I cannot help the way I am'. That may be true in a human sense, but it is a straightforward denial of the power of God's Holy Spirit, one of whose responsibilities is to give us the self-control that we find so hard to achieve in our own strength. Without the Holy Spirit we will never have the power consistently to make the right moral choices, to react with love when we might otherwise lose our temper, and be content with God's plan for our lives instead of being eaten up by greed and selfish ambition.

It *is* possible for God to control our language, our morals, our relationships, and indeed every single area of our lives. But the Holy Spirit is very sensitive to *our* spiritual desires. He will not force His power upon us, but when we call upon Him, He will give us the strength to cope with whatever our personal situation may be. When we have a moral choice, for example, there is a battle in our minds as to whether we should submit to sin or maintain our Christian standards. The Holy Spirit will always give us the strength to win through – if we choose to ask Him. But we can choose to go our own way and deliberately ignore the Holy Spirit's promptings. It is not a sin to be tempted. But it is a sin to grieve the Holy Spirit by losing our self-control.

The object of this chapter has not been to list all the characteristics you need so that you can assess the problems you face and select the characteristics you are going to apply to the situation in hand! I know it sounds silly, but that is often what people think that living the Christian life is all about. It is certainly not the freedom which God has called us to and is a trap which the devil would love you to fall into.

For many years I lived as a Christian with the fruit of the Spirit seeming more like a judgment on the reality of my own faith as opposed to being the normal expression of my Christian life. I had to admit that love, joy, peace, patience, kindness, goodness, faithfulness, humility and self-control were not qualities that came naturally and I even doubted whether or not I was a real Christian!

It was only when I read the Good News Bible for the first time that I really understood what this important bit of Christian teaching was all about. For in this translation it clearly states that, '*The Holy Spirit produces* love, joy, peace etc'. I suddenly realised that it is impossible for me, a sinner, to produce good fruit out of a heart that is sinful, and that it is the work of the Holy Spirit to produce these fruits in my life. My responsibility is simply to be obedient to the voice of the Holy Spirit within, knowing that He will give me the strength to become what, of myself, I know is impossible. The key lies in that word 'obedience'.

In almost every book of the Bible there are lessons to be learnt from the problems encountered by men and women who were not prepared to be obedient to God. And, equally, when people were obedient to His leading, often at some personal cost, we see how God blessed them, sometimes in quite amazing ways. Because disobedience would appear to give us some short-term benefits we deceive ourselves into thinking it is expedient not to listen to the voice of God within us – sometimes with disastrous long-term consequences.

What I am saying, therefore, is this, and it will bear repeating: whatever your situation, if you *are* sensitive in your heart to the Holy Spirit's influence, He *will* lead you into a course of action or behaviour which is in accordance with the Christian standard of living which God is longing to see expressed in your life. There is much more about this and the whole subject of finding God's will for your life in the last chapter.

The Holy Spirit will encourage you along right pathways. It is up to you to listen to His voice and be obedient. The essence of sin is disobedience. And if you do decide to be disobedient at any point you will probably be aware of the fact and feel a sense of guilt. If that should happen do not let the devil kid you that the game's up and your Christian life is over. It is only because you are a Christian that you are so aware of the battle that is going on. God has promised us that 'if we sin, He is faithful and just and (because of Jesus) will cleanse us from all unrighteousness'. Let that scripture be a constant encouragement to living the Christian life. When you fall, get up and keep going. 'Be faithful unto death', said Paul, 'and God will reward you with the crown of life'.

Chapter 6

Gift-Wrapped Power

The Gifts of the Spirit in Action

Peter was a fisherman. He was skilled at sailing boats, mending nets and catching fish. He was a rough working man. He was *not* a public speaker. But on the Day of Pentecost it was Peter who preached a sermon which was full of sound teaching, persuasive arguments and convicting power. As a result three thousand people were converted and the Christian church began to grow.

Something quite amazing had happened in Peter's life. After Jesus had been raised from the dead, He told His followers to wait for God the Father to send them the Holy Spirit. In obedience to what Jesus had said they were waiting and praying together and all who were present in that Upper Room saw and felt the power of God as the Holy Spirit came upon them. They were all liberated in their spirits to praise and worship God in new languages that God had given them (which were understandable to the foreign visitors who were present in Jerusalem at the time).

For three years the disciples had followed Jesus. They believed in Him and all that He had said. But without His daily presence they were helpless. When the Holy Spirit was given to the church, the disciples and all the followers of Jesus who had been waiting in the Upper Room were, by the power of the Holy Spirit, given the empowering life of Christ.

God gave His Holy Spirit to the whole church, but when it came to explaining what was happening to the crowds that had gathered outside in Jerusalem, only Peter got up to preach. The Holy Spirit had given to Peter 'the gift of preaching', so that when he opened his mouth to speak, his words had an authority and convicting power which was not from Peter's mind and lips but from God speaking through him. The gift was instantaneously received and immediately applied.

Shortly after this Peter and John were entering the Temple and a lame beggar called out to them for money. Peter had none, but said to the man, 'In the name of Jesus Christ of Nazareth I order you to get up and walk'. Peter knew what Jesus would have done in a similar situation so, in faith, Peter stretched out his hand to the man, who was instantly healed. Peter had, therefore, also received and used a gift of healing.

Preaching and healing are just two of the gifts which the Holy Spirit gives to God's people. It was through the use of these special gifts of the Holy Spirit that the church was able to grow and cope with the many difficult situations which it had to face during its formative years. Once good Christian doctrine and teaching was established, however, the use of some of these gifts gradually declined in favour of acquired experience and a developing tradition, although throughout the ages there have always been a number of Christians who have been open to the power of God being directed through them in this way.

It is only in relatively recent years, however, that a larger section of the church has come to appreciate that God still gives these gifts to His people and that He wants us to use them effectively for Him. Those churches which have moved in this direction are usually known as charismatic (the word charismatic is taken from a Greek word which now has the special meaning 'gifted by God'). A phrase which you may also hear is 'charismatic renewal'.

This means the renewal which has come in the life of many church fellowships which use the gifts of the Spirit in their ministry.

The question of the importance of the use of spiritual gifts in the ministry of today's church has sadly become a source of disagreement amongst some Christians. Perhaps it should be said at this point, therefore, that the three qualities most needed by Christians on both sides of the discussion are love, patience and wisdom. *Love* of their brothers and sisters in Christ with whom they may not agree on all issues. *Patience* as they wait upon God for His encouragement and guidance. And the *wisdom* to see that their own viewpoint must remain balanced. Sometimes people adopt an extreme position in order to emphasise the distinctive characteristics of their viewpoint. They are then in danger of not being able to support from the scriptures the views they are forced to express!

Whilst there is still some disagreement on these issues, there is now a much wider appreciation by the whole church that God has been at work in and through the charismatic renewal, and that the blessings God has brought to the church through it are for everyone to enjoy.

We saw in the last chapter how God's Holy Spirit will develop the fruit of the Spirit (characteristics of God) in the lives of all Christians who are willing to be obedient to the Spirit's promptings. We saw, too, that these characteristics are not necessarily acquired instantaneously, but that it takes time for our lives to be so changed that our behaviour is always in keeping with the will of God.

This contrasts sharply with the gifts of the Spirit, for a gift is not something that we acquire slowly but that we receive immediately. And when God chooses to give a Christian one of His gifts then that gift is available for use immediately, and can be exercised without having to wait for it to grow and mature. This is the reason why, sometimes, new Christians, in whom the fruit of the Spirit is not strongly evident, can, nevertheless, exercise some of the powerful gifts of the Spirit. In time God will ensure that there is a balance between the fruit and the gifts. It is older Christians that need to be patient during the intervening period! So, don't be frightened of using the gifts of the Spirit – even if you are a new Christian. Thank God for any gift you are given and use it in the most loving and gracious way you know.

We saw in Chapter 4 how the local fellowship of Christians is the Body of Christ in the community. The fellowship is made up of many different people and it is important that this fellowship as a whole should have (and use) all the gifts it needs for its ministry to be effective. A body would be of little use with six left feet and no arms! Equally a fellowship of Christians would find it difficult to cope if all (or none) of its members had the gift of preaching!

When the members of a church fellowship are open to all that God wants to do in and through them, then it is the Holy Spirit's responsibility to ensure that in the fellowship as a whole there is a wise balance of the gifts in use. That is not to say that once a person has received a particular gift he cannot receive another at a different time or for another situation, but it does seem to be the case that once a person has been given a gift to use in the context of the local fellowship, God continues to use that person in the practice of that gift.

Some people exercise several gifts, whilst others are given a special ministry in the use of only one of the gifts. God's will is sovereign, so there is no need to be frustrated or jealous if someone else appears to have more attractive gifts than your own. In God's eyes how we use what God has given us is much more important than what we have been given.

So far in this chapter we have talked generally about the gifts, referred to the new languages given to the followers of Jesus at Pentecost (known as the gift of tongues) and given illustrations of two of the gifts in use – preaching and healing. If you are not yet familiar with them all you'll probably be wondering by now just what the other gifts are and how they can be used in the life of your local church.

Before we do look at individual gifts, however, it is important to appreciate the differences between the natural God-given abilities that people have and the supernatural gifts which Christians receive from the Holy Spirit. Everyone is good at certain things. We might describe a musician, for example, by saying that he is 'a gifted pianist'; that means that the person concerned has been given by God special abilities in this particular area which are his to use throughout his life. God does not force His will on to anyone, so He doesn't say, 'here is a gift, but you can only use it if you worship me'. No, God has given us free-will as to how we use the things that He has given.

As Christians we should submit our talents and abilities to God to be used as He pleases. Sometimes He will take the natural gifts that a person has and sanctify these by confirming the use of that gift in the life of His church. The natural gift then becomes a gift of the Spirit.

At other times, however, God may choose to give a professional musician, who is undeniably gifted, a completely different gift for use in the life of the church. The one danger of people, who are very able in a particular area of life, using that ability in the life of the church is that they are then open to the temptation of doing God's work in the strength of their own experience and not in the power of God. Pride, whether or not it is recognised as such, could interfere with the spiritual ministry of the fellowship.

For example, if there is a banker or an accountant in the congregation, he is often asked to be the church treasurer. That may be right if the individual concerned has truly submitted his gifts and abilities to the Lordship of Christ. But the principles of Christian giving are often at variance with the conventional secular methods of raising and spending money, and it may be hard for a church to be spiritual in the conduct of its financial affairs if the man at the helm of the finances is not sensitive to God's law of supply and demand! God wants us to trust Him, and Him alone. That doesn't mean to say we shouldn't use the abilities that God has given us in the life of His church but we should be particularly on our guard against both spiritual insensitivity as to how God wants us to use those gifts, and pride.

There are several passages of scripture which contain references to the gifts of the Spirit. In the Acts of the Apostles there are specific references to them in use. In his letters to the Romans (Chapter 12), the Corinthians (1 Corinthians Chapters 12 to 14) and the Ephesians (Chapter 4) Paul describes various gifts, explains his own use of them and gives advice as to their practice. There are many different gifts and none of the lists given in these references is intended to be exhaustive. Within his advice Paul indicates that the gifts are always given to individuals, but all his teaching, about the gifts, refers to them being used in the local church fellowship.

There are very sound reasons for encouraging Christians to let God use their gifts *in the fellowship of the church*. For Satan specialises in deceiving people into rebellion against God by giving counterfeit gifts to people who have not submitted their lives to the Lordship of Jesus Christ. (That is why you will hear of Spiritualists, and even Satanists, carrying out healings. What actually happens in these cases is that people are sometimes healed, genuinely, of their physical condition, but spiritually they become blinded to the truth and exchange their physical condition for spiritual darkness.) It is extremely important, therefore, that the gifts of the Spirit, which God gives to His people, should be exercised in the context of a local church fellowship so that they may be tested and confirmed for use in and through the Body of Christ.

There are three different types of gifts referred to in the scriptures – those involving speech, action and knowledge. They are all gifts of power because they can only be exercised in the power of the Holy Spirit. If we attempt to exercise a gift of the Holy Spirit in human strength and with human understanding the effect of our spiritual service will be detrimental to the life of the church.

Gifts of Speech

We have already referred to the *gift of tongues* whereby an individual is given, by the Holy Spirit, a new language in which to worship and praise God. The gift of tongues is, unfortunately, the source of quite a bit of controversy. The subject has, sometimes, caused confusion and alarm amongst new, and even mature, Christians.

In the New Testament, the gift of tongues was first used on the day of Pentecost, as described in Acts 2. The Holy Spirit was dramatically given to the first Christians in Jerusalem and one of the immediate effects was that they began to praise God in other languages. Foreign visitors heard them and recognised their own languages being spoken.

It is clear that the use of tongues continued in the life of the early church. For in the first epistle to the Corinthians, Paul was writing to Christians who obviously possessed and valued this particular gift. He stated that he valued the gift also and that its use should never be forbidden. But he also warned the Corinthian Christians against insisting that everybody *must* have this, or any other, of the spiritual gifts.

In recent years a growing number of Christians have claimed to exercise the gift of tongues and some church fellowships stress its importance. It can be a way in which a person finds release in praising God. It is also used to pray definitely for situations, which the Holy Spirit knows all about, but about which not enough is known to be specific in prayer in one's own language.

Other Christians do seriously doubt whether the tongues people use today are the same as those described in the New Testament. You can meet equally convinced and sincere Christians who, on the one hand, urge everyone to ask for and use the gift of tongues, or, on the other hand, warn fellow believers to steer clear of the whole area!

I believe that the healthy thing for all Christians is to be free from anxiety on these matters. They should not allow themselves to be made to feel that they are missing out on something that God has to offer. God is the giver of all spiritual gifts – it is His business as to what gifts we should individually have. On the other hand it is important that we should keep ourselves open to anything that our heavenly Father should wish to give us and the gift of tongues should not be excluded from our openness.

The second gift of speech is the *gift of interpretation*. This gift is obviously necessary if what is said by one person using the gift of tongues needs to be understood by the rest of the fellowship. A person with the gift of interpretation is able to hear a word from the Lord spoken by another Christian in an unknown language and then speak the meaning directly to those present. This is not a process of translation, but simply trusting the Holy Spirit to give the interpreter the right words. The gift of interpretation is often confirmed in a fellowship by more than one person present being given the same interpretation.

The third gift of speech is the *gift of prophecy*. Prophecy in this context is not foretelling the future but simply proclaiming directly to God's people, in the language that they understand, the specific word of God for those people at that time. Peter's sermon on the day of Pentecost was a prophetic word from God to those who were listening. Prophecy, therefore, is often an important ingredient of preaching.

Both *preaching* and *teaching* are important gifts – they are vital ministries which the church must use if its people are to mature and grow. But how important it is that those who are asked to fulfil teaching and preaching responsibilities should be those who are equipped with these precious gifts of communication!

Some Christians are given a gift of being able to share their faith with non-Christians in such a way that others are brought into a living relationship with Jesus Christ – the *gift of evangelism*. It is not only preachers that are sometimes evangelists – the best evangelists are often those who can talk naturally about the Lord in a one-to-one conversation. Some do have a *gift of conversation* through which they are able to talk lovingly to others, and with genuine interest in them. By winning the confidence of others in this way they are able to find out any particular needs that lie hidden beneath the surface so that help can be given.

To some Christians God has given a particular *gift of prayer* so that their time can be effectively used to bring before God the needs of others. This sort of prayer is called intercession, for through it man intercedes with God on behalf of someone else. Encouraging others is a precious and selfless activity which all Christians should learn. But some are given a particular *gift of encouragement* to use in the church so that others will begin to realise their God-given potential as men and women in the body of Christ. In 'the world' there are very few encouragers – in 'the church' there should be many!

God wants to use all these gifts to build up the body of Christ and make it an effective vehicle for communicating His love to the world. They are all precious and none is to be considered more or less important than the others.

Gifts of Action

All the gifts of the Spirit that we have already looked at require faith and action in order to put them into practice. But, set apart from these special verbal gifts are those which result in situations being supernaturally changed as a result of the gift being exercised, the principal ones being *healing*, *miracles* and *faith*.

The gift most commonly encountered in this category is the *gift of healing*. There is nothing more dramatic in action than a person being healed of a physical illness. And Jesus specifically promised that believers would lay their hands on the sick and they would be healed.

All Christians can be used to pray for those who are sick, but the Holy Spirit does give to some individuals special healing gifts. These gifts are sometimes specific to particular sorts of conditions and at other times general for all conditions. For example, it is not unusual for someone to be frequently used by God to heal people with psychiatric problems but for that same person not to have any special gifts when praying for physical ailments.

The gift of healing, like tongues, is often a gift that causes confusion and misunderstanding, most specifically because not all people prayed for are healed and there does not appear to be any constant pattern or rule that can be applied. There *are* situations where a specific sin that is unconfessed, or lack of faith, or some other known reason prevents someone from being healed. But even allowing for all such obvious reasons, it is confusing to see two people with similar conditions, one of whom is healed and the other is not. All that one can do is recognise that God's will is sovereign and that He knows what He is doing.

The *gift of miracles* refers to the supernatural hand of God at work in circumstances which would normally be considered to be in contravention of the natural laws which control the universe. Jesus feeding five thousand people with five loaves and two small fish is a good example. Also a series of apparent coincidences which are used by God to fulfil His will can be as much a miracle as a supernatural event.

The *gift of faith* is exercised when man takes action in response to the prompting of God's Holy Spirit in circumstances which makes God's intervention necessary for the action to be successful. For example, the gift of faith is a necessary counterpart to the gift of healing. Without faith in God's intervention the gift of healing has no potential!

Less dramatic, but nevertheless equally important, gifts of action are: *helping others, administration, serving, giving hospitality*, etc. These practical Christian ministries are often vital weapons used by the Holy Spirit in the cause of evangelism. There are many people, who were eventually converted to Christ, who were first made to think about God when they were on the receiving end of some divinely inspired practical ministry. It takes as much faith to go out of one's way to help a person, because God has told you to do it, as it does for someone with the gift of healing to lay their hands upon somebody who is sick! Many of these practical ministries are things which we, as Christians, should all be involved in. But some people find that one particular area of Christian service becomes especially important in their life, and in their case this is then one of their gifts from God rather than part of their general witness and service.

Gifts of Knowledge
Knowledge in this specific sense refers to divinely revealed information – information that is given by God to an individual for use in his personal ministry in the life of the Body of Christ. Knowledge, wisdom and discernment are the three gifts in this category referred to in the scriptures.

The *gift of knowledge* has many applications in the life of the church. Consider someone who has an effective counselling ministry. He will, as he converses with the person needing help, be listening with one ear (as it were) directed towards the individual and the other directed to God. The Holy Spirit will frequently reveal to the counsellor information without which it would not be possible for any real progress to be made. For example, a person may be wanting help, without actually being willing to reveal something embarrassing which is at the root of the problem. In that situation God may either tell the counsellor exactly what the problem is, or guide him as to the right questions to ask. Or it may be that something has happened in the individual's life which is so deeply buried in the past that it is not considered by the individual to be important. With the gift of knowledge God will bring that to the surface so that the root source can be prayed about and the individual healed as a result. There are many situations in Christian ministry where the gift of knowledge makes it possible for an effective ministry to be fulfilled.

Closely allied to the gift of knowledge is the gift of *wisdom*. Wisdom is something that King Solomon asked for. He recognised that in leading a nation there would be many situations where his wisdom would be called for. He anticipated that without God's wisdom he would make mistakes and he knew that on his own he would struggle and be an ineffective king. Not all the situations which the church faces are easy to understand and there are many occasions when an individual with the gift of wisdom can see God's solution to a problem so that the Body of Christ may effectively fulfil the will of God.

We have referred several times in this book to the work of Satan, and how he desires to make people join with him in his rebellion against God. One of the methods he uses is to allow an evil spirit to either oppress a person constantly or even to take up residence in that person, in which case we say that the individual is possessed. Unfortunately the consequences of such oppression or possession are not always easily recognisable as being from this source. All that one is aware of is that there is a problem in the life of the person concerned.

The *gift of discernment* enables a church to recognise when it is that a problem is caused by a direct attack from Satan or one of his evil spirits. Once the source of a problem in a person's life is identified as being due to this cause it is possible for the *gift of deliverance* (expulsion of the evil spirit) to be exercised in faith so that the individual may be restored and brought to a living faith in Jesus Christ. The ministry of deliverance is a specialised one and it is particularly important that individuals should not attempt to launch into this ministry on their own but should always exercise it in and through the fellowship of the Body of Christ.

When a person receives Jesus Christ as Lord and is filled with the Holy Spirit he is able to receive those gifts which God wants him to have and to use at that time. It is not an issue for new Christians to get hung up on, but it is important to realise that the power of God is not restricted to those who are older in the faith!

God wants you to be effective *now* for Him. He wants your life to be powerful as you take your place in the life of the Body of Christ. Prayerfully ask God to show you the gifts He wants you to use. Do not be jealous of other people's gifts. And, when you believe you know the gifts that God is giving you, test them out in the life of the local fellowship so that you will have the encouragement of them being confirmed for use.

In Christ you're not only a new person but you're God's special agent in a world that is hostile to Him. He wants you to have at your disposal all the resources you will need to fulfil your commission.

Chapter 7

Where Do I Go From Here?

Finding and Following God's
Will for My Life

God has promised that Christians can know His will for their lives. And that is a promise you can claim for yourself. But, like most promises found in the scriptures, there is a condition attached to its fulfilment!

In The Good News Bible, part of the second verse of Romans 12 is translated 'you will be able to know the will of God, what is good and is pleasing to Him and is perfect'. Knowing that, and carrying it out, is the key to living as a Christian, for the centre of God's will is also the place of both peace and power.

But this promise, telling us that we can know the will of God, comes in the middle of one of the most important passages in the New Testament. It is from a long letter that Paul wrote to his Christian friends in the city of Rome. And as with any short passage of scripture, if we want to really understand its meaning we must try and understand the context in which it was written.

In the first part of the letter Paul explains in simple terms about the sinfulness of man and the holiness of God. How Jesus died in our place so that we could be put right with God, and how when God looks at those who have trusted their lives to Jesus all that He sees is the purity of Jesus; our sins are completely blotted out. He tells us that

God's salvation is for all who believe – irrespective of who they are – and affirms that all who confess that Jesus Christ is Lord, and believe that God raised Him from the dead, will be saved from the eternal judgment of God upon their sinful lives.

That, in a nutshell, is what the first eleven chapters of Romans are all about. But when he comes to chapter 12 Paul challenges his readers to think about what their reactions to all this should be. He is intensely concerned that all Christians should live practical Christian lives which are purposeful in the context of their relationship with God and, therefore, meaningful to those around who do not know Him.

Paul makes his appeal to us in the only terms he knows will work – the same terms on which Jesus came to earth for the sake of mankind – the terms of sacrifice. But Paul is not thinking about a dead animal sacrifice lying on an altar of stone, nor is he thinking about Christians prematurely offering themselves to be crucified for the sake of following in Jesus's footsteps (although in all ages there are Christians who have been called to sacrifice their lives as martyrs). No, the words Paul uses are these: 'Offer yourselves as a *living sacrifice* to God, dedicated to His service and pleasing to Him. This is the true worship that you should offer'.

Earlier in this book we talked about worship as 'offering to God that which is worthwhile and worthy of Him'. The most we can give Him is the life we have to live; so Paul concludes that the very highest form of worship is giving ourselves unreservedly to Him. And he implies that if we really want to live the Christian life to the full, and enter into the joy of serving God, then we don't have any alternative but to accept for ourselves these terms of true worship.

So what exactly does it mean to be a living sacrifice? Let's look a little harder at these two words.

A *sacrifice* is something that is surrendered in favour of a higher cause. The something that Paul is talking about is the rest of your life. Now, Paul is not suggesting that you should necessarily withdraw from all the activities of life and sacrifice yourself in this way – you would then be effectively dead as far as serving God in the world is concerned, for you would be unavailable to Him.

With the word *living* in front of the word *sacrifice* the meaning you then have is this: living positively for God, spending your life doing those things that He wants you to do, and day-by-day considering His will to be more important than your own desires. Now, don't make the mistake of thinking that God wants to take away from you the enjoyment of all the good things of life! The fact of the matter is that we were made in the image of God and it is only when we are living our lives in His service and doing those things which please Him that we can ever enjoy live to the very full! So a Christian who is committed to being a living sacrifice can expect to enjoy life far more than those who try to create human happiness out of a series of self-oriented activities.

So, we have established that the only way to really enjoy life is to spend our days doing God's will, which begs the ultimate question, 'Just how do we know what God's will for our lives is?' Fortunately, Paul goes on to tell us.

His answer, however, is a bit of a riddle, but it is a riddle with a solution, albeit a challenging one! These are Paul's words: 'Do not let yourselves be conformed to the standards of this world, but let God transform you inwardly by a complete change of your mind'. I can hear you saying, 'That's no answer, I'm as much in the dark now as I was earlier!' So we will divide the answer into its two parts.

Firstly, 'Do not let yourselves be conformed to the standards of this world'. J. B. Phillips translates this phrase in a very helpful way. He says, 'Don't let the world around you squeeze you into its own mould'. For it is true that the world is a mould with its own standards and conventions which are sometimes very different from those we would expect of a Christian.

88

For example, the world would sometimes conclude that it is not a sin to do wrong, only a sin to be found out! The shopkeeper who would prosecute a shoplifter puts himself into the same category of offender when he fills in his tax return and deliberately overlooks some income he should be declaring. Stealing time from one's employer – not giving a fair day's work for the agreed wage is an 'acceptable sin' and when it comes to making a personal telephone call on the office 'phone – well, who cares anyway, everybody does it? And what about the so-called 'legitimate perks' of the job – helping oneself to some materials or stock items which belong to the firm? This, in simple terms, is theft, but a surprisingly large section of the population do not consider this to be wrong. Then, what about personal relationships – pre-marital (and often extra-marital) sexual relations are an increasingly common pattern of behaviour, and homosexual relationships by both men and women are often considered to be acceptable alternatives, provided that both partners agree to the arrangement.

One could go on, but the above should be sufficient for you to appreciate that the world does have its own set of standards. Paul encourages us not to drop our Christian standards of behaviour just to gain acceptance by the world, but to realise that a Christian is set apart by and for God and no matter how much temporal pleasure may be obtained by indulging in the behaviour of the world, at the end of the day that which has been obtained or experienced in ways which are disobedient to God will turn sour and reap its own bitter harvest.

Sin is only pleasurable for a short time. Once its glamorous facade has been dropped and we see sin for what it is, all that we have left is a tarnished memory which will never satisfy.

The second part of Paul's answer is: 'Let God transform you inwardly by a complete change of your mind'. There is no way whatsoever in which you can purify yourself from the standards of the world. The more you try the more attractive the world's offerings seem to be! There is only one answer, and that is to let your mind be radically changed from the inside!

We are not talking here about conversion – you will remember from Chapter 1 that at conversion your spirit, which was dead to God because of sin, was born again. But in the years that preceded your conversion some pretty deep ruts were carved in your life as a result of the lifestyle you then led and habits you formed, and becoming a Christian has not instantaneously filled those ruts and given you a smooth road to walk on – old habits die hard!

As a Christian, however, you do have a big difference in your favour – Jesus. Keep your eyes on Him and by the power of God's Holy Spirit you will have the strength to walk on the right road. God has promised to put your feet down on a secure path. Take Him at His word and trust Him to do it – don't think that you know a better way, trying to hang on to some of the world's standards and at the same time keeping on the straight and narrow way. You can't, and you will fail. So don't try.

Unless you hand over every area of your life to His control you will never be totally at peace with both God and yourself. With some Christians the hand-over to God is a bit like a war of attrition as bit by bit they release areas of their life to His control! Others, from the word 'go', see that their only hope is God and that there's no point in hanging on to anything. It is often those who have, as it were, been won into the Kingdom from the very jaws of hell who become the inextinguishable fire brands for God.

It can be much harder for those who have been brought up to believe that to be a Christian is to live up to an 'acceptable standard of behaviour'. For this is frequently complemented by an 'acceptable compromise with the world' and when they are converted it is hard for them to see the chasm they crossed when they became Christians and recognise the dramatic about-turn that is necessary from all their double-standards.

The time has come, therefore, for a gloves-off showdown. Because Jesus died for you, and you have trusted Him, you will one day enjoy heaven's glory as a redeemed sinner. Your name *is* written in what John, in the book of Revelation, calls 'the Lamb's Book of Life'. (Jesus is often referred to as the Lamb of God.) BUT, for Christians that is not the end of the matter. For it is abundantly clear from many different scriptures that one day we will each have to account to God for the life we have lived since we were converted. Jesus is referred to as the 'one and only foundation' for life. And what we do with our life is expressed by Paul as building on that foundation.

Paul describes the 'judgment of Christians' in terms of a fire which will burn all that is built on the foundation. The things that are worthless (the dross of our Christian lives) will be destroyed. But the untouched gold, silver and precious stones (representing those things which are of eternal value) will be a measure of the quality of our Christian life. (1 Corinthians 3:11–15). We do, therefore, have a responsibility before God for the way we live as Christians and what we build on the foundation that God gave us in Christ.

If you really understand this and let its truth burn into your life you will have no difficulty in both desiring to know the will of God for you and in being willing to obey the day-by-day promptings of God's Holy Spirit.

It is at this point that the phrase which is often used to describe the Christian life, 'service which is perfect freedom', comes sharply into focus. For, on the face of it, serving someone else within an apparent straight-jacket of moral behaviour is certainly not perfect freedom! On the contrary, however, it *is* perfect freedom to continually live one's life in response to the promptings of God's Holy Spirit knowing that He never could, nor would, lead you into a pathway which runs contrary to God's standards of living or His will for you.

With God in absolute control you can, once and for all, relax. Not into an attitude of 'it doesn't really matter how I behave now that I'm a Christian, I can always be forgiven!', but into a totally new concept of living, with God at the helm of your life; knowing that sin is not just a case of breaking God's moral law, but, in a much wider sense, being disobedient to the voice of God's Holy Spirit.

God's promise, that you can know the will of God, really is for you. The way to claim it is simply to hand the key to *every* department of your life over to Him – so that God can and will transform you inwardly by a complete change of your mind. And as we saw in Chapter Five, that is not something you can do for yourself, but is the work of God's Holy Spirit.

We do not naturally demonstrate love, joy, peace, patience, kindness, goodness, faithfulness, humility and self-control. Our natural personality is much more likely to display the characteristics of immorality, idolatory, enmity, lust, jealousy, anger, selfish ambition and other such things with which Paul contrasts the fruit of God's Holy Spirit in your life (Galatians 5:19–22).

When Jesus went back to heaven He promised not to leave His disciples alone. On the day of Pentecost God fulfilled that promise when He gave the Holy Spirit to the church. And by 'the church' you will now understand that we do not mean the local denominational building, but the people of God who, together, are called the Body of Christ. And that means you too!

Without the Holy Spirit the disciples were powerless to live the Christian life. With the Holy Spirit they were bold enough to leave the shelter of the upper room and in the first few chapters of Acts you can read of the amazing things that happened. You are just like the disciples – without the Holy Spirit you, too, are powerless to live the Christian life. In your own strength you can only live within the limits set by whatever framework you choose to restrain your behaviour, and even then, when faced with some test or temptation which stretches those limits, you will find it hard to justify staying within them.

With the Holy Spirit you're completely free to be God's man or woman in today's world. Free to be obedient to that quiet but insistent voice, confident that He will never lead you into paths which are contrary to God's law. And confident, too, that when obeying Him you will be putting your feet down in life on the perfect pathway that God has mapped out for you.

Just one word of caution though, do not let this freedom be an excuse for not reading the Bible and understanding God's written word. Unless you know what God's word says, Satan could deceive you into a false course of action. God's Holy Spirit, who inspired the writing of the Bible, *cannot* direct you along paths which are contrary to its teaching. So, always be alert to that harmonious balance between the written word of God and the prompting of God's Holy Spirit in your heart.

So far in this chapter it has all been theory. I do not pretend that there are no problems in converting spiritual theory into day-by-day practice. For example, you may be thinking right now about your job, your recreation, your relationships, your home and family – all sorts of circumstances where you know there is conflict and in which you would love to see God's will for you worked out in practice.

Paul's advice to people who are considering a major change in direction in their lives is, stay where you are until God moves you out. And that is still very sound advice. So, you must first start to apply the principles we have talked about in this book within your present situation – be patient, be obedient, let God's Holy Spirit develop in you the characteristics of God Himself.

This may mean, for example, that in your job you will stop agreeing to any small areas of deceit which are an accepted practice in your work. The stand you take will probably be noticed; you may be commended by your employer for your honesty, or, conversely, he may not like it if you will not do things which are wrong, but which would be to his advantage. You'll be surprised at how quickly circumstances are changed when we start living out the consequences of being a Christian in our working environment. Do not worry, God will use those changed circumstances to move you into that place which is the centre of His will for you.

Then, again, you may have been living intimately with your girlfriend or boyfriend. Putting your relationship right will either cost you the relationship or so deepen your bond that your partner will be made to think about what has happened. You will need to be praying very hard for him or her. God will either then bless your relationship or you will go your separate ways – either way you will then be free to be obedient to God's Holy Spirit.

What if you are married to a person you no longer love? God's word tells us that marriage is for life and we shouldn't therefore be looking for the superficially easy way out via the divorce courts. Your first course of action is simply to ask the Holy Spirit to give you God's love for your partner so that you will be able to behave towards him or her in accordance with God's plan for married life. Your life will be enriched, and if you have children, they too, will notice the difference and start to flourish under your influence.

You may be in a financial mess with all sorts of problems brimming round your ears. Tell the Lord about the situation. Never let the pressures encourage you to succumb to the temptation to be dishonest – even if only to cover up the mess in front of friends. The Lord will honour you as you let Him take control and give Him first place in your life. His word says: 'For them that honour me I will honour'.

One could go on, but whatever situation you are facing, however difficult it may be, God is sufficient to meet your needs. Hand the whole lot over to Him, be obedient to the Holy Spirit's leading and the written word of God. Seek the advice of older Christians. Trust God and you will very quickly find that He is Lord of every situation.

It is clear from all this that living the Christian life can be costly. But it is also exciting and challenging. Some may think it too costly, but do not let that deter you. It is the only life which promises love in exchange for hate, joy in exchange for unhappiness and peace in exchange for despair or distress.

Stand up, walk tall – you are a child of the King. He is your Heavenly Father, He loves you and cares for you. Go out and live for Him – the Kingdom of God really *will* come within *your* life and the lives of all those who are influenced by you.

Chapter 8

Postscript

You have come to the end of the book. Well, not quite, there is one more chapter. For it is possible that much of what you have read is outside your experience and you now realise that even though you believe in God and know a lot about Him, you don't actually know Him for yourself. If that is you, then this last chapter could change your life.

No one else can choose what you do with your life. That is your decision – and whilst you may think that your responsibilities end with yourself and your immediate friends or family – they don't. Your ultimate responsibility is to God. That is why when David confessed the sins he had committed against other people, he knew that his words of confession had to be to God Himself (Psalm 51). He admitted to God, 'against you – only against you – have I sinned'. He realised that in doing things that were not in keeping with the character of God he was actually sinning against the God who had made him.

We have all sinned – and we have all, therefore, not just sinned against other people but against God Himself. How you respond to this truth *is* your responsibility. God made you in His own image. He wanted to enjoy a living relationship with you. He is not particularly concerned that people should only believe that He exists, for as the Bible tells us, even the devil believes in the existence of God!

You may have believed in God all your life, even tried to

live your life as you thought God would want you to – but deep down, you, and probably only you, know that your eternal expectations are not built on a secure foundation but on the shaky hope that God will welcome you into His Kingdom because you have been good enough.

The most famous of all Easter hymns talks about Jesus in this way:

> There was no other good enough
> To pay the price of sin.
> He only could unlock the gates
> Of heaven and let us in.

And that is the truth contained in the Bible. Belief in God is not enough. The Bible tells us unmistakably that the way we live *is* important, but it also tells us that this must be an expression of the life of Christ within and not camouflage (no matter how impressive the camouflage may be!) for a heart that is proud and independent of God. A religious way of life may satisfy our desires to be thought important in the sight of God, it may even look impressive in the eyes of the world, but what man does to please God is nothing when compared to what God has already done for man through Jesus Christ.

The Bible tells us that Jesus is the only foundation for life. It is only through Jesus that our sins can be forgiven. It is only through Jesus that we can know God. It is only through Jesus that we can know God's perfect will for our lives. And it is only the will of God for us which will free us from the daily burden of having to tailor our lives to fit the moral or religious straight-jacket we have chosen to wear.

If you were not interested in God you would not have read this book. So, be honest – both with yourself and with Him. Do you only believe about God: or do you really know Him? Do you only believe that when you sin, you sin against other people: or have you confessed that you have sinned against God Himself? Do you only believe that Jesus was the Son of God and lived on earth and died for mankind: or have you said goodbye to all your independent pride and trusted God that Jesus died for you? Are you only thinking that you *might* enjoy eternal life: or do you have personal assurance in your heart that your sins are forgiven; that Jesus Christ is now the foundation of your whole life; and that, for you, eternal life has already begun?

The journey of a thousand miles really does begin with a single step. Whatever stage of life you're at, whoever you are, however much education you have had, knowing God begins in the same way. You can start now and here's how:

1. Go back to Chapter 1 and read it carefully from beginning to end. It describes what happened to those who became Christians before reading this book.
2. Then ask yourself if you would like to receive Jesus Christ into your own life so that you will not only believe about Him but trust your life to Him.
3. If the answer is yes, read the following prayer through and think about what it will mean to you. If having done that your answer is still yes, pray the prayer to God yourself – either out loud or quietly in your heart.

Father God, I now realise that in my own strength I can never be good enough to enjoy a personal relationship with you. I confess that I am a sinner and that I have sinned against you. I now know that you sent Jesus to show me how much you love me and to die on the cross for me.

Father, I ask you to forgive me. Lord Jesus I ask you to come into my life *now*. Without reserve I hand over to you all that I am and all that I have, so that you can make me what you want me to be, and you can live your life through me.

Father, I ask that you will fill me with your Holy Spirit so that in my life I will start to demonstrate the characteristics of God and that I will have your power to live the Christian life. Thank you Lord for a new beginning. Amen.

4. If you have prayed this prayer and really meant it Jesus has entered your life. Now take your Bible and look up John 5:24. There words of Jesus will assure you that if you have trusted Christ you already have eternal life. The new life of Christ is now yours.

5. Thank God for what He has done for you. Thank Jesus for coming into your life and becoming a sure foundation. If you are a member of a church fellowship tell your friends. If not, find a local church and share with other Christians what God has done for you.

6. Now read the rest of the book again, knowing that the Holy Spirit will help you to understand the things that you need to know as you work out the consequences of the living Christ being alive in you! God will bless you as you live for Him.

Appendices

Appendix A
Relevant Bible References

Chapter 1

Eternal Life: Jn. 10:10; Jn. 3:14–16; Jn. 5:24; Jn. 10:27–28, Rom. 5:21; Rom. 6:23; 1 Jn. 5:11–13.

New birth: Jn. 3:3–8; 1 Jn. 3:9–10; Titus 3:5.

Trinity of Man: 1 Thess. 5:23.

God is Spirit: Jn. 4:24.

Man has a spirit: Gen. 1:26; Gen. 2:7; 1 Cor. 2:11.

Everyone's body will die: Rom. 5:12; Rom. 8:10.

The soul is eternal: Rev. 20:11–15; Lk. 16:19–31.

Everyone's spirit is dead to God: Eph. 2:1–5; Rom. 3:23.

Consequences of sin – eternal separation from God: Rom. 6:21–23; Rev. 20:11–15; Rev. 21:27.

Jesus' death for us: Matt. 27:45–50; Mk. 15:33–41; Lk. 23:44–49; Jn. 19:28–30; Matt. 20:28; 1 Tim. 2:5 and 6; Rom. 4:25; Rom. 5:6–11; 2 Cor. 5:21.

Resurrection of Jesus: Matt. 28:1–10; Mk. 16:1–8; Lk. 24:1–12; Jn. 20:1–10; Acts 2:22–35; 1 Cor. 15:1–23.

Our response to God: Acts 4:12; 1 Jn. 2:2; Rom. 10:9.

God's Spirit brings life to our spirit: Jn. 6:63; Rom. 5:10; Rom. 8:10–11; Titus 3:5–8.

Our relationship with God is restored: Rom. 3:21–26; Rom. 5:1–11; 1 Jn. 3:1–2; Deut. 6:5; Jn. 17:3.

Food for growth: 1 Cor. 3:2; 1 Tim. 4:7–8.

Fatherhood of God: Gal. 3–26; Rom. 8:15–17.

A new foundation: Matt. 7:24–27; Lk. 6:47–49; 1 Cor. 3:11; 2 Tim. 2:19.

A new hope: Ps. 71:5, Col. 1:5; Rom. 12:12.

Chapter 2

All things made new in Christ: 2 Cor. 5:17.

Dealing with sin as a Christian: 1 Jn. 1:9; Rom. 6:15–18.

Peter's denial of Jesus: Mk. 14:23–30 and 66–72.

Peter's sermon at Pentecost: Acts 2.

Relationships: 1 Cor. 6:19 and 20.

> *With parents*: Exod. 20:12; Eph. 6.

> *In marriage*: Gen. 2:20–24; Eph. 5:22–33; 1 Cor. 7:1–16.

> *Sex outside marriage forbidden*: 1. Cor. 6:13–18; Eph. 5:5–8; 1 Thess. 4:3–4.

> *Boyfriend/girlfriend*: 2 Cor. 6:14.

Time: Eph. 5:14–17; Col. 4:5.

Sundays (Sabbath): Deut. 5:12–15; Exod. 20:8; Mk. 2:27; Lk. 6:5.

Entertainment: Rom. 8:5–6; Gal. 6:7–8; Phil. 4:8–9.

Language: Col. 4:6; James 3:1–12; Deut. 5:11; Exod. 20:7.

Money:

> *Tithing*: Num. 18:21–26; Deut. 14:22–24; Deut. 14:28–29.

> *Freewill offerings*: Deut. 16:10; Ezra 3:5 and 8:28; 1 Tim. 6:10.

Truth: Jn. 14:6 and 16:13; 1 Jn. 1:5–7.

Occult: Deut. 18:14–15; Matt. 4:8–10; Gen. 3:1–15; Lk. 10–18; Jn. 8:42–47.

> *Commandment against idolatry*: Exod. 20:3; Deut. 5:7.

> *Spiritualism forbidden*: Deut. 18:10–13.

Chapter 3

Pharisees' misuse of God's law: Matt. 6:1–7; Matt. 12:1–8; Matt. 15:1–9; Mk. 7:1–13.

Jesus' condemnation of Pharisees: Matt. 23:1–39; Lk. 11:39–52; Lk. 16:15–17.

Jesus praying alone: Matt. 14:23; Matt. 26:36–46; Mk. 6:46; Lk. 6:12.

Jesus praying publicly: Matt. 11:25–26; Matt. 14:19; Matt.

19:13; Lk. 3:21; 10:21; Lk. 11:1–2; Jn. 11:41–42; 12:50; Jn. 14:16; 16:27; 17:1–26.

Jesus confronts Satan with scripture: Matt. 4:1–11; Mk. 1:12–23; Lk. 4:1–13.

Jesus quotes or refers to Old Testament scripture:
    Matt.: 4:1–11; 5:27–48; 12:3–8; 12:39–42; 19:4–9; 19:17–19; 21:16; 22:42; 22:31–32; 22:43–45; 24:15; 24:37–39; 26:31; 26:54–56.
    Mark: 1:12–13; 2:25–28; 6:6–13; 9:12–13; 10:3–9; 10:9; 11:17; 12:24–27; 12:35–37; 13:14; 14:21; 14:27.
    Luke: 4:1–13; 4:18–21: 4:25–27; 6:3–4; 7:27; 11:29–32; 17:26–29; 18:19–20; 18:31–33; 20:17–18; 20:41–44; 22:37; 24:44–48.
    John: 3:14; 5:39–47; 6:32; 6:49; 6:58; 6:45; 7:19–24; 8:17; 8:56; 10:34–35; 13:18; 15:25.

Importance of scripture: 2 Tim. 3:16; Ps. 119 espec. 9–16; 105; James 1:22–25.

Jesus teaches about prayer: Matt. 6:1–18; Mk. 11:23–26; Lk. 11:1–13.

Confession: 1 Jn. 1:9; Matt. 6:14–15.

The coming of God's kingdom:
    Jesus's Teaching: Matt. 24 and 25; Mk. 13:1–37; Lk. 21:5–36.
    Parables: Matt. 13:1-52.
    Defeat of Satan: Heb. 2:4.
    Testing by God: James 1:3; 1 Pet. 1:6–7.

Chapter 4

The Church – The Body of Christ: 1 Cor. 12:12–27; Eph. 1:22–23; 5:23; Col. 1:18.

Life in the Local Church:
    Worship: Ps. 95:6; Jn. 4:23 and 24; Rom. 12:1 and 2.
    Praise: Ps. 92:1 and 2; Ps. 50:23.
    Teaching: 2 Tim. 3:16; Eph. 4:11; 1 Tim. 2:2.
    Prayer: 1 Tim. 2:1–3.
    Fellowship: Phil. 2:1–5; 1 Jn. 1:6–7; 1 Jn. 2:9–11.
    Breaking of bread: Matt. 26:26–29; Lk. 22:17–20; Jn.

13:12–30; 1 Cor. 11:23–24.
Baptism: Matt. 28:19; Mk. 16:15–16; Jn. 3:22; Acts 2:38.
Service: Matt. 20:26; 1 Cor. 10:31; Phil. 2:3 and 4.

Chapter 5

The fruit of the Spirit: Gal. 5:22–23; Jn. 15:1–8; 2 Pet. 1:5–8.
Love: Jn. 3:16; Rom. 5:8; 1 Jn. 3:1.
Joy: Phil. 4:4; 4:10–13.
Peace:
>*With God*: Phil. 4:7; Rom 5; Jn. 14:27; Eph. 2:13–14; 1 Jn. 1:9; Isaiah 1:18.
>*With others*: Jn. 23:34; Eph. 6:12; Matt. 5:44; Lk. 6:27; James 5:16; 1 Thess. 5:10, 1 Cor. 12:12-25.
>*With ourselves*: Rom. 8; Rom. 8:28–39; 1 Jn. 3:20–22; Eph. 1:6–7.

Patience: Ps. 27:14; Prov. 3:5–6; Rom. 5:3–5; James 1:2–4.
Kindness/Goodness: Phil. 4:8; Gal. 5:19–23; Lk. 10:33.
Faithfulness: 1 Thess. 5:24; 2 Thess. 3:3; Rev. 2:10.
Humility: Phil. 2:5–8.
Self-control: Rom. 8:5–6; Gal. 5:25.

Chapter 6

Day of Pentecost: Acts Ch. 2.
Promise of the Spirit: Jn. 14:15–18; 25–26; 15:26.
Peter preaches: Acts 2:14–41.
Lame man healed: Acts 3:1–10.
God gives spiritual gifts: Mark 16:14–18; Rom. 12:4–8; 1 Cor. 12–14; Eph. 4:7–16; 1 Pet. 4:10–11; Heb. 2:3–4; 1 Cor. 2:14.
References to specific gifts:
Speech:
>*Tongues: private*: 1 Cor. 14:18; 1 Cor. 12:10, 28.
>>*public*: Acts 2:4–12; 1 Cor. 14:1–28.
>*Interpretation*: 1 Cor. 14:13; 26–28; 1 Cor. 12:10.

Prophecy: 1 Cor. 14:1–5; 29–33, Eph. 4:11; 1 Cor. 12:10, 28.
Teaching: Eph. 4:11.
Preaching: 1 Pet. 4:10.
Evangelism: Eph. 4:11.
References to specific gifts:
Action:
Healing: Acts 3:1–10; 1 Cor. 12:9; 1 Cor. 12:28.
Miracles: 1 Cor. 12:10, 28.
Faith: 1 Cor. 12:9.
Helps: 1 Cor. 12:28.
Administration: 1 Cor. 12:28.
Serving: 1 Pet. 4:10.
Hospitality: 1 Pet. 4:9.
Knowledge:
Word of knowledge: 1 Cor. 12:8.
Wisdom: 1 Cor. 12:8.
Discernment: 1 Cor. 12:10.

Chapter 7

Knowing God's will: Rom. 12:2; Col. 3:15.
Man in God's image: Gen. 12:16.
Living God's way: John 10:10.
Consequences of continuing in sin: Rom. 1:18–32; Rom. 6:21–23; Prov. 14:12.
Christians, set apart for God: 1 Cor. 3:16–17; 1 Cor. 6:19–20.
God's ability to keep us: Ps. 40:2; Ps. 16:11; Phil. 1:6.
Lamb's book of life: Rev. 13:8; 21:27; 20:11–15.
Judgment of Christians: 1 Cor. 3:9–15; 2 Cor. 5:9 and 10.
Promise of the Holy Spirit: Jn. 14:16–17; Jn. 15–26.
Coming of the Holy Spirit: Acts 2 onwards.
Advice to those considering change: 1 Cor. 7:17–24.

Appendix B

A Short Guide to Christian Denominations

In Chapter 4 we saw how differing views on Christian doctrine and church organisation led to the establishment of denominational structures. The principal denominations are described below. These descriptions are factual and non-critical. They are intended as a guide for new Christians who may be confused by the church scene they first encounter.

1. Church of England (Anglican)

This is 'the established church' in England. The word 'established' refers to the fact that the church, with the Queen as its nominal head, is the official Christian expression of the Government. Bishops, for example, are appointed by the Queen on the recommendation of the Government, though, in practice, recommendations are made to the Government by the Anglican hierarchy.

The Church of England has related and similar churches all over the world (members of the worldwide Anglican communion). Anglican churches are sometimes called 'Episcopal', which refers to the fact that they are governed by Bishops and Archbishops.

The whole of the British Isles is divided into parishes. A parish is a local area of land centred on a community such as a village or part of a town. Each parish has at least one church. Sometimes a parish church also has a daughter church in a different part of the parish; there can also be two or more churches in a parish if the present-day parish has resulted from the amalgamation of several parishes which no longer justify an independent existence. The clergyman responsible for each parish is usually called the Vicar, sometimes the Rector.

Parishes are grouped into deaneries. Each deanery is presided over by a Rural Dean. He, in turn, is responsible to an Archdeacon for his deanery. Several deaneries are grouped together into what is known as a diocese and at the head of each diocese is a Bishop with the Archdeacons being responsible to the Bishop for their group of deaneries.

In England, the Bishops are responsible to one of the two Archbishops (York and Canterbury) according to the geographical location of their diocese. In each diocese there are also Assistant or Suffragan Bishops who can carry out responsibilities on behalf of the Diocesan Bishop but do not have diocesan authority. Membership of the Church of England is achieved by being baptized (by any of the clergy) and subsequently confirmed (by the laying-on of hands by a Bishop).

The form of worship in Anglican churches is significantly different from that in most other Protestant denominations. The services usually follow the form laid down in a prayer book. The two books most commonly encountered are:

(a) 1662. The Book of Common Prayer (BCP) and

(b) 1980. Alternative Service Book (ASB).

The BCP contains some very beautiful language, but it is seventeenth-century English and new Christians, especially, find it hard to understand and follow. The ASB was introduced in 1980, as an alternative to the BCP. The language is modern as well as reverent. But the ASB is only an alternative to the BCP and not all churches use it.

2. Roman Catholic

Whilst the organisation of the Roman Catholic church is similar to the Anglican church, with its structure of Priests, Bishops and Archbishops, there are significant differences in belief which have created division between the Roman church and all the other Protestant (non-Catholic) churches. For example, Roman Catholics believe that under certain conditions the Pope's judgments can be infallible. Some of the other significant differences between Roman Catholics and Protestants are their beliefs relating to the mass (holy communion), the emphasis placed on confession to God through a priest and the special significance they attach to Mary the mother of Jesus.

There are many similarities between the liturgical forms of service of the Anglican and Roman Catholic churches.

3. Methodist

In the eighteenth century the Church of England, as it then was, could not cope with the special life, teaching and ministry of John Wesley and his followers. Whilst Wesley himself lived and died an Anglican priest, his ministry was rejected by the established church and he and his followers were forced to meet elsewhere. As a result they formed their own church societies and the preaching houses that were built for John Wesley and his associate preachers became the first buildings of the new Methodist denomination. Methodists originally acquired their name from the jibe John Wesley collected in his Oxford days as a result of being so methodical in his religious duties.

The Methodist Church as a denomination flourished rapidly but Methodism had many local variants, each one having all the hallmarks of an independent denomination! It wasn't until the Act of Union in 1932 that most of the branches of the Methodist Church became united under the one denominational name. On a worldwide scale the Methodist Church is now the largest of the 'free churches'. The word 'free' now simply means Protestant and 'not established' (in the Anglican sense).

Methodist Church services do not follow a prayer book pattern. They are a combination of hymns, prayers (not usually from a prayer book) and preaching. One of the
110

unique features of Methodism is the large and important role played by the lay-people in the organisation and ministry of the denomination. For example, the majority of Methodist church services are conducted by lay preachers (members of local congregations who, though not ordained, exercise a preaching ministry in their local churches). Each local church (society) is part of a circuit of churches. The circuit is controlled by a superintendent minister who may have a number of other ministers to help him. The circuits are grouped into districts which are under the jurisdiction of the District Chairman. His responsibility in Methodism has something in common with that of a bishop in the Anglican church.

The organising and governing body of Methodism is the Annual Conference which meets to discuss the affairs of the church. Each year the Conference is presided over by a new President and the President of the Methodist Conference is the effective head of the Methodist Church during his term of office.

4. Baptist Churches

The particular characteristic of Baptist churches is their practice of Believers' Baptism by immersion. The Roman, Anglican and Methodist churches normally baptize babies as infants, but the Baptist church (as well as some other free churches) dedicate their babies to God as infants and then wait until they are mature enough to personally confess their faith in Jesus Christ before they are baptized. Hence the name 'Believers' Baptism'.

A Baptist church minister is assisted in his work by a team of lay people elected from the congregation and called Deacons. Most Baptist churches are members of the Baptist Union. There is very little control exercised over individual churches however by the Baptist Union and most local fellowships are autonomous in the way they exercise their ministry and conduct their worship.

5. United Reformed Church (URC)

The United Reformed Church is a 'new' denomination in that it only came into being in 1972. It was formed by an amalgamation of the Congregational Church in England and Wales with the Presbyterian Church of England. In 1981 they were joined by the Re-formed Association of the Churches of Christ.

The denomination is old, however, in that Congregational and Presbyterian churches have a long tradition going back to the Reformation. The Congregational name refers to the relative independence in local church affairs exercised by each congregation within the denomination. The word Presbyterian is taken from the word Presbyter. This is a literal translation of a Greek word used in the New Testament for the leaders of a church. Presbyterianism, therefore, refers to the system of government of a church by Presbyters. The Presbyterian churches of Scotland (Church of Scotland), Ireland and Wales remain independent of the URC.

The governing body of the URC is the General Assembly which meets each year under the direction of a National Moderator, who, like the President of the Methodist Conference is only in office for twelve months. Regionally the URC is divided into twelve provinces each of which is in the care of a Provincial Moderator, to whom individual ministers are responsible for the care of their local congregation.

6. Lutheran and Reformed Churches

The Reformation resulted in a division between the Roman Catholic Church and the emerging Protestant Christians. Initially the Protestants followed the teachings of either Luther or Calvin.

Those that followed Luther became established in what are now known as Lutheran churches. Although there are not many such churches in the United Kingdom, on a worldwide scale the Lutheran church is significant. The Lutheran church is now the established church in
112

Scandinavia and is the major Protestant church in Germany. There are some similarities between the Lutheran churches and those in the Anglican communion.

A number of different denominations arose among those Protestants who followed Calvin. They have a broadly similar doctrine and are collectively known as Reformed. The reformed churches have distanced themselves further from the Roman Catholic position than the Lutherans, especially with regard to church organisation and structure, their doctrine of holy communion and their attitude to the scriptures.

7. Pentecostals

In Chapter 6 it was mentioned that there have always been some Christians who have believed in the continuing use of the gifts of the Spirit. For obvious reasons some of these Christians have been known as Pentecostals. Since the beginning of this century a number of Pentecostal Churches have been formed. Some are completely independent but, in the United Kingdom, most are included under one of the following groupings: Apostolic Churches, Assemblies of God or the Elim Pentecostal Churches.

8. Salvation Army

The Salvation Army is one of the most respected of the independent Christian organisations. Their combination of a powerful evangelical witness with radical social concern has earned admiration far beyond the confines of their military style structure.

It was started by the Rev. William Booth who broke away from the Methodist church to put into practice less conventional methods of reaching the poor for Christ. By 1876 the movement had acquired the name Salvation Army and subsequently became quickly established in all parts of the world. There is a branch of the Salvation Army in most towns in the United Kingdom. The music for their services usually incorporates wind instruments, drums and tambourines.

9. Christian Brethren

Early in the nineteenth century the Christian Brethren were established as a break-away from the Roman Catholic church in Dublin. Their principal concern was to establish the authority of scripture, a New Testament pattern for church organisation and the unity of all believers. An assembly in the United Kingdom was established in Plymouth – hence the name Plymouth Brethren which has usually been associated with the denomination.

One branch of the Christian Brethren became exclusive and in an effort to cut themselves off from the world they also cut themselves off from other Christians in their own denomination. Those Brethren Churches that are not exclusive are often referred to as Open Brethren.

10. House-Churches

Whilst the house-churches are not a denomination in the normally accepted sense of that word, they are the fastest growing group of churches in the United Kingdom. They usually meet in people's houses or hire school halls, and place great emphasis on the authority of scripture and on the work of the Holy Spirit.

11. Other Smaller Denominations

There are a number of other smaller denominations with representation in the United Kingdom. Examples of these are the Fellowship of Independent Evangelical Churches (FIEC), the Church of the Nazarene, the various African and West Indian churches, Free Methodists, independent Congregational Churches, etc.

LETTERS FOR AUNTY FLO

A light hearted approach to the serious subject of Radical Discipleship, with a set of discussion starters for groups.

- David wanted to buy an expensive car, God made him buy a banger.
- David thought peace meant no war, God told him about shalom.
- David thought only other people were racist, God made him think again.
- David went along with the crowd, God helped him go anti-flow

Graham Young is Regional Youth Officer for the Methodist Church in the North of England. He has worked with Christian Aid and the Shaftesbury Project, and is also involved with Traidcraft and the Frontier Youth Trust.

SHARING YOUR FAITH

'I'm too reserved for witnessing'
'My life is witnessing for Christ; that's enough'

Are you one of the casualties who have set out to share your faith and failed? Witnessing is, in the best sense of the word, **easy**. Canned presentations or forced attitudes are not necessary. Selwyn Hughes shows that when you are able to **be yourself** rather than trying to be what you are not, then sharing your faith becomes a delight, not a duty. The only really effective witnessing is natural – witnessing consistent with who and what you are.

This book is a must for all those who want to get out from under the 'guilt trap' brought on by failure in sharing their faith. Selwyn Hughes regards it as his most important book to date.

If you have enjoyed reading this book and would like to see our complete catalogue, ask at your nearest Christian bookshop for one or write directly to MARSHALL PICKERING COMMUNICATIONS at the address below.

If you have ideas for new Christian books or other products please write to us too!

MARSHALL PICKERING COMMUNICATIONS
3 Beggarwood Lane
Basingstoke
Hants RG23 7LP
England